THE PALACES OF BRITAIN

John Adair

SAPERE
BOOKS

THE ROYAL
PALACES OF
BRITAIN

Published by Sapere Books.

20 Windermere Drive, Leeds, England, LS17 7UZ,
United Kingdom

saperebooks.com

ISBN: 978-1-80055-105-3.

For Thea

TABLE OF CONTENTS

INTRODUCTION

A Procession of Palaces

'More like unto a paradise than any earthly habitation,' wrote a contemporary who saw Hampton Court in the year when Henry VIII acquired it from Cardinal Wolsey. The palace in its heyday was much more than a roof over the crowned head. Great, stately and sumptuous buildings, with wide courts and large, richly furnished rooms, palaces were tents pitched in the imagination between heaven and earth, inhabited by persons divinely appointed to rule.

Because palaces are so much a product of the imagination they escape a narrow definition. Certainly not all royal residences were palaces. This book does not even attempt to list all the castles, manor houses and residences that have belonged at one time or another to the various royal families: between 1066 and 1485 alone they amounted to eighty-six 'king's houses' and 150 castles. Instead the focus is upon ten palaces which stand out on account of their splendid past and stately present: the Tower of London, Windsor Castle, Hampton Court, Whitehall, St James's, Greenwich, the Royal Pavilion at Brighton, Holyrood, Kensington and Buckingham Palace.

The histories of these palaces overlap considerably and there are many others — some destroyed, some now far removed from royal connection — that were part of the overall story, which begins at the Norman Conquest. By virtue of winning the Battle of Hastings in 1066, Duke William of Normandy acquired all the residences of his Saxon royal predecessors. In medieval Latin manuscripts a residence owned and occupied by the king was usually called *domus regis*, 'king's house'. The word *palatium*, 'palace', which appears much later, comes from the Palatine, chief of seven hills in Rome, where the first emperor Augustus built his house. Tiberius, Nero and later Caesars so extended and adorned the buildings that they eventually covered the whole hill and became a byword throughout the civilized world for vastness and splendour. In the West the old Roman imperial tradition received new life in the year 800 when the pope crowned Charlemagne as the first Holy Roman Emperor. The monarchs of Western Christendom — tribal kings by origin — gradually followed his example: as they became national kings they looked back to imperial Rome for models of how to live.

William the Conqueror was a notable exponent of this aspect of the common Latin culture. Like his Saxon predecessors, William donned his state crown and robes to attend mass on high festivals. Among his English residences, according to the *Anglo-Saxon Chronicle*, he chose three — Winchester, Westminster and Gloucester — for the ancient ritual of wearing his crown on the great festival days of Easter, Whitsun and Christmas. That was, perhaps, a fundamental meaning of a palace: the place where the sovereign was seen crowned in all his glory with the full panoply of state about him. Thus a palace centred on a hall large enough to accommodate the throng of archbishops and bishops, abbots and earls, thegns and knights — all potential troublemakers in Church and State — who needed such periodic reminders of the king's pre-eminence. The high gold crown, rich clothes and colourful crowd of supporters, together with the splendour of the palace itself, were intended to create a sense of awe in the minds of the beholders. No wonder that some simple cleric, nurtured on church wall paintings of Christ crowned in glory, and overcome by the presence of majesty, had burst out, 'Behold, I see God!' as he gazed at King William passing in great dignity before him. It is said that Archbishop Lanfranc rebuked the man, but the King may well have been secretly pleased, for he and his successors certainly saw themselves as God's vicegerents set over the English — and they were determined to be housed accordingly.

Of the three Saxon palaces mentioned by the chronicler, two gradually drop out of the story. The western palace of Gloucester fell first from favour. Like their Saxon predecessors, the Norman kings kept their main treasury in the royal buildings at Winchester, the ancient capital of Wessex, but their plan to erect a new and better palace did not materialize. Winchester's prestige as a principal city was waning and in the reigns of the last two or three Anglo-Saxon kings Englishmen had come to look upon London as their capital or, at least, the most important place in the kingdom. Over the next few centuries this factor inevitably worked to give Westminster the primacy at the expense of Winchester.

During Saxon times the Benedictine abbey on the Isle of Thorns, a low marshy section of the Thames bank overgrown with hawthorn bushes and brambles, became known as the minster in the west of London — or Westminster. Marauding Danes pillaged and burnt the monastery buildings several times. Edward the Confessor undertook to restore the community's property, but first he had built for himself a palace between the abbey and the Thames. The Bayeux Tapestry portrays him in it — the earliest surviving picture of an English king in his palace. In the Tapestry the hall and the royal apartments seem to form part of a single building, not standing apart as in the older Saxon palaces. The King's bedchamber, where he is shown dying, is depicted above the hall, which suggests that it may have been on the first floor adjoining the dais end. The neighbouring Westminster Abbey was eventually consecrated on 28 December 1065, sixteen years after the masons had cut the first stones. King Edward, who wore his crown at Westminster on Christmas day, had become too ill to attend the ceremony and he died a few days later.

King William I and his court often celebrated the great festivals in Edward the Confessor's palace. At Whitsuntide in 1068 his consort Matilda — daughter of the Count of Flanders and a descendant of Alfred the Great — was crowned at Westminster. Although the Conqueror continued the building works on the palace left unfinished by the Confessor, it was his son William Rufus who raised Westminster Hall. The largest hall in England and perhaps in Europe, it measured 240 feet in length and almost 67 feet in width. The royal workmen completed it after two years in 1099, the year when the Crusaders captured Jerusalem. Even so, it fell far short of William II's original idea of a great hall for a new Norman palace to the south. 'No, it is a mere bedchamber to what I intended to build,' retorted William to one of his knights, who had ventured the opinion that it was too large for daily use. Yet on New Year's Day in 1237 King Henry III could entertain over 6,000 poor men, women and children to a feast under its low roof. Thus the royal household, a few hundred at most, must indeed have been lost in the vast hall as they sat down to their dinner served on long oak tables.

If Westminster Hall, with its soaring roof and painted angels, impressed the majesty of kings upon the minds of subjects, there were other buildings in the palace designed to produce much the same effect. Henry III transformed the old wooden hall and bedchamber where Edward the Confessor died, the spiritual heart of the palace, into a stone-built hall known as the Painted Chamber. It was so called because his artists adorned the flat ceiling with angels and covered the walls with more rich blue, gold and red paintings of divine favours bestowed upon kings, drawn from such sources as the Wars of the Maccabees. Above the royal bed one mural depicted the coronation of Edward the Confessor, while others showed some miraculous incidents from his life, themes also carved in stone round his shrine in the abbey next door. Another wall painting showed a crowned English monarch, holding a shield emblazoned with the golden leopards of England in his left hand and a wooden club in his right, standing firmly on the back of a cringing subject. It was entitled 'The Triumph of Meekness over Anger'. Even the window ledges carried suitable Biblical texts.

Eventually Westminster Hall began to lose its grandeur; there were no embankments on the river, and when flood waters surged into the hall in 1236 men rowed boats into the middle of it, 'being forced to ride to their chambers'. In a later year the flood waters suddenly receded from the hall, leaving behind a sea of mud with silver fish gasping and tossing upon it. Vandalism also played its part. In 1267 a mob forced a way into the palace and 'drank up the king's wine, brake the glass windows and defaced the windows most disorderly'.

Richard II's architect, Henry Yevele, who began the work of restoration in 1394, raised the height of the old walls and fortified them with the strong buttresses we see today. Then he removed the double line of pillars which had supported the roof of the Norman building and installed the magnificent hammer-beam roof of English oak adorned with carved angels. This elaborate canopy, spanning in one arch a width of nearly 70 feet, is still the largest timber roof in Europe unsupported by pillars. As a single timber hammer-post in it weighs about three and a half tons, the roof was truly a marvel of medieval engineering. To celebrate its completion, King Richard employed a small army of cooks to regale thousands of guests at a series of splendid banquets.

By this time other palaces had sprung up from the seeds of royal castles that William the Conqueror had planted like dragons' teeth round his capital. In a corner of London itself, the Tower of London now stood massively guarding the river gates, a fortified palace of forbidding strength. Either in the White Tower or in the adjoining palace hall Richard II sealed his abdication, which led to the transfer of the crown from the Plantagenets to the House of Lancaster. To the west of London stood Windsor Castle, another fortified palace. The Conqueror began building it upon a hill above the Thames two miles upstream from a Saxon palace called Kingsbury. Other Norman castles in the ring, notably Guildford and Berkhamsted, saw kings and queens frequently in residence in their princely buildings, but they never became fully-fledged palaces.

During the Middle Ages and long afterwards the court was almost constantly on the move, as the monarch visited his castles and manor houses or stayed with his more wealthy subjects. In 1300, for example, King Edward I and his court moved house seventy-six times! In the days before newspapers, radio or television it was important for royalty to be seen in the shires. Moreover, this constant movement allowed the burden of feeding, and indeed feasting, a small army of courtiers, officials and domestics, together with their horses, oxen and sumpter mules, to be shared by more than one locality.

The incessant royal progresses threw a considerable strain on the courtiers. A restlessly energetic and unpredictable monarch such as Henry II could make their life a purgatory. 'If the King promised to remain in a place for that day — and especially when he has announced his intention by the mouth of a herald — he is sure to upset all the arrangements by departing early in the morning,' complained Peter de Blois. 'As a result, you see men dashing around as if they were mad, beating their pack-horses, running their carts into one another — in short, giving a lively imitation of hell. If, on the other hand, the King orders an early start, he is certain to change his mind, and you can take it for granted that he will sleep until midday. Then you will see the pack-horses loaded and waiting, the carts prepared, the courtiers dozing, traders fretting and everyone grumbling.' Worse still, Henry would sometimes turn off the road to stop for the night where there was only one house for himself. 'I believe that in truth he took delight in seeing what a fix he put us in,' added Peter. He had witnessed his fellow courtiers arguing with drawn swords over a hovel among the dripping trees 'that it would disgrace pigs to fight for'. Walter Map, an itinerant justice who had more than his share of travelling with Henry II, once declared that life in such a court was not hell, 'but as nearly like it as a horse's shoe is like a mare's'.

Although Westminster remained the principal royal palace until it was first damaged by fire in 1512, it gave English kings little scope for one of their ruling passions — hunting. Gradually they acquired country houses or hunting lodges in southern and midland England, such as Clarendon in Wiltshire, where they could chase stags, deer and wild boars to their hearts' content. The most celebrated of them was Woodstock in Oxfordshire, which the Conqueror's youngest son, Henry I, built for himself, together with a great deer park enclosed by a wall 7 miles long. Later kings enlarged this stone hunting lodge until it became a miniature palace in the country.

Much medieval romantic legend surrounds 'Fair Rosamund', the mistress of Henry II, who is said to have lived at Woodstock Palace. In 1165 Henry built a stone house round a spring which flowed below the palace on the south-east hillside and helped to fill the fishponds (now submerged by the lake made for Blenheim Palace). Round it he added cloisters and bowers, to produce a delightful little water-palace alive with the sound of water splashing down through its courts. Such was 'the king's high chamber by the pool', better known to history as 'Rosamund's Bower'.

After poor Rosamund, who was said to have been poisoned by Henry's wife, Eleanor, the house is perhaps most associated with another young woman with a less tragic life before her. Princess Elizabeth was held prisoner at Woodstock in 1554 during the reign of her half-sister Queen Mary Tudor. While there Elizabeth saw a milkmaid singing in the fields, which prompted her to say that she would rather be that milkmaid, for 'her case was better and life more merrier than was hers'. She inscribed some verses about her imprisonment on the wall, signed 'Elizabeth a prisoner'. Underneath these lines she added: 'Much suspected of me, but nothing proved can be'.

Woodstock slowly fell into disrepair. King James I visited it in 1603, much to the disgust of his minister Robert Cecil, who found its proximity to the marshy springs in the valley unwholesome and the situation generally unpleasant, 'for there is no savour but of cows and pigs'. Hardly an evocation of paradise!

The early Tudors were great builders and acquirers of palaces, such as Eltham in Kent and Sheen on the Surrey banks of the Thames. In particular, Henry VII began the work of renovating Placentia, the old house of Humphrey, Duke of Gloucester, which had come into his possession and which was renamed Greenwich. Takeovers brought his son two more palaces. After Westminster had been ruined by fire, Henry VIII induced Cardinal Wolsey to give him York Place, the London residence of the See of York, which the King renamed as Whitehall. In the same manner he acquired Wolsey's country palace at Hampton.

Yet Henry's appetite for fair buildings, like his lust for pretty women, remained unsatiated by these conquests. The King acquired or bought other properties, notably the hospital of St James's in the fields near Whitehall, the manor of Oatlands in Surrey, and the manor of Hatfield in Hertfordshire. The main attraction of these places was the hunting, but they served their turn as homes for Henry's wives or nurseries for his children. St James's he planned as a country palace for Anne Boleyn. The red-brick palace of Oatlands, which spread over 14 acres, was intended originally for Anne of Cleves, but Henry found her unacceptable as a consort. Oatlands was finally completed for Katharine Parr to live in. Orchards of apple, pear and cherry trees, brought there from the gardens of Chertsey Abbey, must have made it a beautiful sight in blossom time.

Hatfield Palace, built originally by his father's minister Cardinal Morton (in his capacity as Bishop of Ely), came into Henry's possession by compulsory exchange. At Hatfield, on the morning of 17 November 1558, Elizabeth heard the news that she was queen. She stood up from her seat below an oak tree that still leans in the park, then knelt down and repeated before the booted-and-spurred councillors the words she had just read in her psalter: 'This is the Lord's doing; it is marvellous in our eyes.'

Perhaps the most spectacular of Henry's palaces was Nonsuch. Even for his contemporaries it possessed a dreamlike quality. For us it is among 'the cloud capp'd towers, the gorgeous palaces' which Prospero in *The Tempest* foretold would dissolve and 'like this insubstantial pageant faded, leave not a rack behind'. For not a stone of that palace without equal — Non Such — now stands. Even to build it Henry VIII had destroyed a village called Cuddington in Surrey. Envy probably inspired this palace, for Henry was determined not to be overshadowed by Francis I, the creator of the Château de Chambord. Feeding like a cannibal upon stones from Merton Priory, the extraordinary palace grew up round the familiar ground plan of two courts, an outer and an inner one. Two lofty and well-proportioned octagonal towers, the fourth storeys projecting out like drums and set with a band of wide windows, stood on either flank of the long gallery facing the garden.

Artists and craftsmen of the stamp of Nicholas Bellin, an Italian borrowed from Fontainebleau, worked to embellish the interior of the inner court and the house itself with all the tricks and glories of Renaissance art, as if it was the vestibule of paradise.

Playing water, sparkling in the sunlight, is an essential ingredient in any such vision, and the eyes of the visitor in the inner court were drawn to a splendid white marble fountain. A stone white horse dominated it. Three figures of the Graces arm-in-arm poured water into a basin, which two golden griffins supported. Great plaster reliefs, 'full of Kings, Caesars, Sciences, Gods', painted in white and gold, stood round the court in frames of French slate. On the far side of the court the figure of Henry VIII sat enthroned in splendour, not out of place in this pantheon of Mount Olympus. In the gardens round the house the Labours of Hercules was one of the scenes portrayed in the marble sculptures, a fitting subject for 'the majestic lord who broke the bonds of Rome' to contemplate in his old age.

When King Henry died in 1547, nine years after a small army of workmen had begun work, the spectacular inner court had been finished and the rest of the palace was nearing completion. As Nonsuch had no great hall, it has been surmised that Henry probably planned it as a palatial hunting lodge, like Chambord or Fontainebleau. The siting of the banqueting house on the highest part of Nonsuch Park, so that the ladies could watch the hunting in progress from its balconies, certainly supports that idea. Queen Elizabeth clearly enjoyed the extravagance of Nonsuch, but her Stuart successors did not care for it. Eventually Charles II assigned the palace to his mistress Barbara Palmer, Duchess of Cleveland, and later she sold what remained of the house and the park to pay her debts.

The northern kingdom of Scotland contained such palaces as Holyrood, Linlithgow and Falkland, but even they possessed a fortress-like quality about them. Scottish monarchs spent so much of their time in mortal fear of their subjects that it is not surprising they became like hermit crabs in their craggy castles. When King James VI of Scotland succeeded Queen Elizabeth in 1603 he found much to delight him in the palaces he inherited or acquired in England.

James soon exchanged the old episcopal palace of Hatfield House with Robert Cecil for Theobalds, or 'Tibbolds', a house which he had coveted from the day he set eyes upon it on his first triumphant journey south. Cecil's father, Lord Burghley, enlarged Theobalds several times to accommodate Queen Elizabeth's court — she inflicted herself upon her faithful minister no less than twelve times! The Queen had the nerve to suggest even more alterations to her harassed host. 'Upon fault found with the small measure of her chamber (which was in good measure for me),' wrote Lord Burghley rather wearily, 'I was forced to enlarge a room, which need not be envied of any for riches in it.' According to one visitor, so realistically painted were the oak trees lining the walls of this great chamber in the Fountain Court, that when the windows were opened birds flew in from the pleasure gardens and perched themselves on the branches and began to sing. Only a stretch of garden wall remains today of Theobalds, the palace where James died in 1625.

Queens of England always had their own establishments, usually listed in the marriage treaty. For example, James gave Somerset House to his consort, Anne of Denmark. Elizabeth had inherited this noble house in the Strand, built for the Duke of Somerset, who had temporarily ruled the roost as Lord Protector of England in Edward VI's reign. It was said to be the first house in England constructed in the Italian style. Both Queen Anne and the wife of Charles I, Henrietta Maria, lived in Somerset House (renamed Denmark House). Henrietta Maria commissioned Inigo Jones to improve the Tudor house for them. The old tennis court now housed an ornate Roman Catholic chapel, a source of as much offence to her husband's Puritan subjects as the lavishly expensive masques she staged in the hall, in which she appeared herself occasionally in the dress of a man.

Anne of Denmark kept Inigo Jones fairly busy. At Greenwich, he designed for her the Queen's House, a masterpiece of Palladian architecture. At Oatlands Palace, also a gift to the Queen, he built for her a new gatehouse and brick silkworm house in the middle of a large mulberry garden there. For King James he designed the Banqueting House at Whitehall; it stands today as the last survivor of that great

London palace. Rubens adorned the ceiling with some allegorical scenes on canvas which included a portrait of James I as a majestic god. One wonders whether or not Charles I glanced up at the figure of his father in heavenly glory before he stepped out of a window of the Banqueting House onto the high scaffold where the headsman's axe awaited him.

After the Restoration in 1660 his son Charles II found that few of the royal palaces had been well maintained, except those occupied by Oliver Cromwell and his generals. With a sense of history Charles commissioned Sir Christopher Wren to build a palace for him in Winchester, where Saxon and Norman kings had once worn their crowns. Work came to a halt when his successor, James II, ordered Wren to concentrate on the rebuilding of Whitehall. The abandoned buildings served as a prison for French prisoners-of-war and then became a barracks for a regiment of foot until a fire in 1896 rendered them uninhabitable.

The Glorious Revolution of 1688 brought to the throne King William III and Queen Mary II, who ruled as joint sovereigns. Lacking enthusiasm for either Whitehall or St James's, they searched for a new royal residence in the capital where William's asthmatic chest would be untroubled by river fogs. Eventually they purchased from their Secretary of State Nottingham House, near the village of Kensington, and renamed it Kensington Palace. When the great fire of 1698 gutted Whitehall Palace, King William surveyed the smoking ruins next morning and ordered Wren and Nicholas Hawksmoor to prepare plans for a new Whitehall. But Dutch William's heart was never in it and Whitehall became a colony of government ministries. Queen Anne, last of the Stuarts, by contrast liked to live in the red-brick palace of St James's, which enjoyed a heyday now that its London rival, Whitehall, was no more. The Tower, of course, had dropped out of the running centuries earlier; Charles II was the last monarch to sleep a night there, on the eve of his coronation procession through London.

For palaces in their capital the first two Hanoverians contented themselves with St James's and Kensington. Their successor, however, who spoke better English and felt more at home, wanted a family home of his own. After the birth of their first child, George III and Queen Charlotte began to look in earnest for a house with a large private garden, which St James's lacked, and near to the seat of government, which Kensington was not. In 1762 they purchased Buckingham House, and it subsequently became the Queen's official dower house in exchange for Somerset House. By making modest alterations and additions to Buckingham House, George III began the process which led to 'the King's House in Pimlico' becoming the principal royal residence in the capital.

George III had schemes for another palace: a Gothic 'baronial' castle in the grounds — now Kew Gardens — of the old Richmond Palace, where already a succession of follies, temples and pavilions had materialized to fulfil the more capricious dreams of his predecessors. But George became almost blind and mentally ill before his castle was anywhere near completion.

During these dark years his successor ruled as Prince Regent. As Prince of Wales, George IV (as he later became) had inherited Carlton House, which stood in the old shrubbery of St James's beside the Mall. His architect Henry Holland reshaped it into the finest house in London, with lavishly furnished lofty rooms and a great ballroom in the grand French style. A 'tribune' or ceremonial vestibule at the heart of the building and a temple at the gallery end anchored Carlton

House securely in the classical tradition. Yet an exotic Chinese Room hinted at other models in the East, new possibilities that would take root in the Prince Regent's imagination and bear fruit in the onion domes of the Royal Pavilion at Brighton.

While he was Prince of Wales George kept a brilliant court at Carlton House. To pay for it and the bills of living there in his own style he ran up the enormous debt of more than half a million pounds. Parliament, at the request of his father, voted funds to clear the costs of the house, but personal economy was foreign to the Prince's nature. At length, in return for the cancellation of his debts and a higher income, George agreed to marry his plump cousin, Princess Caroline of Brunswick. It was a disastrous marriage, but it fulfilled the immediate purpose. After he became Prince Regent in 1811 Carlton House served George as a London palace. There in 1816 his only child, Princess Charlotte, married Prince Leopold of Saxe-Coburg in the Grand Crimson Drawing Room. Two years earlier, the Prince Regent held some glittering state banquets at Carlton House to celebrate the Allied victories over Napoleon. The Tsar of Russia and the King of Prussia, together with some of their famous generals, sat down at his table.

For some years Carlton House remained the focal point of society in London. Ladies danced the new waltz — that immoral Viennese invention — with their Regency bucks in the Ballroom, while their fathers gambled at *chemin de fer* in the Circular Drawing Room. But when in 1820 the Prince Regent became George IV and inherited Windsor Castle and Buckingham Palace, he had no more use for Carlton House. In 1826 he gave permission for it to be dismantled and sold piecemeal. In Thackeray's words, it 'exists no more than the palace of Nebuchadnezzar'.

After her accession in 1837 Queen Victoria moved from Kensington to Buckingham Palace, henceforth the London home of the sovereign. In five years of marriage to Prince Albert, Queen Victoria had five children. The royal couple wanted a house where family life could be enjoyed in privacy. In 1845 she purchased Osborne House in the Isle of Wight, which became 'the dear little Home' she had sought. Her concept of paradise upon earth reflected the values of her age: it was summed up in her description of Osborne as 'a place of *one's own*, quiet and retired'.

Because the Solent reminded Prince Albert of the Bay of Naples, the new house was built in the style of a Neapolitan villa. The proceeds of the sale of Brighton Pavilion paid for much of the furnishings. In the garden Prince Albert built a 'Swiss Cottage', a chalet imported from Switzerland, where the family could take tea together and the princesses could learn cookery in the spotless kitchen. The children helped with the gardening, each with a personal wheelbarrow and set of tools.

When Prince Albert died in 1861 Osborne became for Victoria a shrine to his memory. Yet she could not escape the burden of being Queen Empress of a growing family of nations, as well as acting as head of a large family of her own. As Osborne lacked a great hall, she found it difficult to entertain her large family of grandchildren there. In 1891 she gave permission for the 'Durbar Room' to be built at the entrance. This Indian hall, richly decorated by Indian craftsmen directed by Bhai Ram Singh, is a relic of that highest pinnacle of British imperial glory, the Queen's title as Empress of India. Here her grandchildren, or the distinguished guests who attended state banquets in Cowes Week, could eat their dinner by electric lights hidden in large blue vases given by Indian merchants at the time of the Golden Jubilee.

Osborne lacked one essential element in the nineteenth-century vision of paradise on earth: it was not set in a wild place. The desire to get back to nature, pioneered by the artists and poets of the Romantic movement, found expression in a delight in wild, rugged or picturesque scenery. The advent of the railways made it possible for Victoria and Albert to indulge this instinctive feeling in Scotland, a land brought alive for the English Victorians by the novels of Sir Walter Scott. In 1848, while the builders were still at work on Osborne, Victoria rented Balmoral House, near Braemar. 'The scenery all around is the finest almost I have seen anywhere,' she wrote. 'It is very wild and solitary, and yet cheerfully and beautifully wooded.' In 1852 she purchased the estate and a new house, designed in the Scottish baronial style by Prince Albert, was built during the next three years and decorated inside with a profusion of pine and an extravagant use of tartan material. 'Every year,' the Queen added, 'my heart becomes more fixed in this dear Paradise and so much so now *all* has become my dearest Albert's own creation… his great taste and the impress of his dear hand have been stamped everywhere.'

Prince Albert bought for his son Edward, Prince of Wales, the Sandringham Estate in Norfolk. In 1870 Edward and his wife Alexandra replaced the existing house with a red-brick mansion in the late Tudor style. Queen Victoria, who visited it for the first time in 1871, noted that the road to it 'lay between commons and plantations of fir trees, rather wild-looking, flat, bleak country, and the house rather near the high-road, a handsome, quite newly built Elizabethan building'. The same architect, Albert Humbert, designed the uncomfortable annexe in gabled Victorian Gothic which the Prince gave to his son George, Duke of York, in 1893. The future George V and his family lived here for thirty-three years. 'Dear old Sandringham,' he once wrote: 'the place I love better than anywhere in the world.'

Queen Elizabeth II lives mainly in Buckingham Palace and Windsor Castle, two palaces supported by the nation. She spends some of her holidays at Sandringham and Balmoral. Like her medieval predecessors, the Queen travels incessantly each year both at home and overseas. In Scotland she can reside at Holyrood, the third palace in use as a royal residence in her realm. The Tower of London, St James's and Kensington are still known officially as palaces, but these are more like courtesy titles. No sovereign has slept in them in recent times. That fact, however, should not diminish the interest with which we approach them and their sister palaces. For history can both restore a royal presence and re-create vanished splendours, so that we share in some measure those feelings of awe, surprise and joy which each palace evoked in its different way.

1: THE TOWER

Ye towers of Julius, London's lasting shame

This late 15th-century image is the earliest surviving non-schematic picture of the Tower of London.

Silver-grey against the skies, the Tower of London has stood massive and immutable for nine centuries. William the Conqueror's great Keep crowns the forbidding fortress of battlemented walls, towers and turrets. Gundulph, Bishop of Rochester, the leading military architect in William's service, built for him the White Tower, so called because it was whitewashed. The lofty walls, which taper from a formidable 15 feet wide at the bottom to 12 feet at the top, were fashioned in Portland stone, but the interiors were lined for the most part with blocks imported from the quarries of Caen, perhaps so that the Norman barons surrounding the Conqueror and his son William Rufus should feel at home.

What did the Tower say about the nature of kingship to those who watched the labourers raising those solid walls ever higher under the watchful eye of Bishop Gundulph? Above all, it proclaimed the dominant strength, the armed might and the permanency of the new Norman dynasty. The native Anglo-Saxons, not least the 'vast and fierce' population of London, did not readily accept their new masters. For the first century of its existence, the Tower stood as a hated symbol of foreign occupation, as menacing to Londoners as, in later days, the Bastille to the French or the Berlin Wall to the East Germans. In the course of time, as the Normans blended into the population, the Tower was attributed to an earlier conqueror, Julius Caesar:

> *Ye towers of Julius, London's lasting shame,*
> *With many a foul and midnight murther fed.*

The Romans had indeed enclosed London with a wall, and the Tower stood in its south-east corner near the Roman bridge spanning the river. Possibly it also occupied the site of the Saxon 'burh', or citadel, which King Alfred built to safeguard London once he recovered it from the Vikings.

Some twenty years after the foundations had been dug, the Tower stood ready for occupation, its white walls standing high above the roofs of the city. Within the limitations of a hall-keep Bishop Gundulph had created a building which contained the essential rooms of a king's dwelling or palace. The royal bedchambers, with their unrivalled views, occupied the top floor. Upon the two storeys below them could be found the Council Chamber, the Chapel of St John, the Banqueting Hall and the royal Privy Chamber. The first king to keep his court there seems to have been Stephen, who celebrated the feast of Whitsuntide in 1140.

King John refortified and repaired the Tower — a timely act, for it was besieged in May 1215 by the barons and citizens of London. It held out until news came of the signing of Magna Carta and then the Archbishop of Canterbury received custody in accordance with the King's agreement. In the following year it was temporarily surrendered to Louis, son of the French king, who led an army into England in support of the baronial cause. The buildings had suffered a considerable battering, yet in 1220 John's successor, Henry III, kept his court at the Tower during Lent, when, inevitably, fish dominated the menus: the bailiffs of Gloucester, for instance, sent 300 lampreys for the royal table. The King relished gingerbread, dates, conger-eels, salmon pasties and herrings — though he considered 'all other fish insipid beside lampreys'.

During Henry's reign and that of his successor, Edward I, the White Tower became the hub of two extended and concentric rings of defences: curtain walls studded with bastion towers and pierced by entrances guarded by strong gatehouses, including a most impressive water-gate on the riverside. The outer moat, flooded with water from the Thames, now enclosed an island of some 12 acres bristling with fortifications. Within the safety of the inner bailey, on the south side of the White Tower, Henry III constructed a range of palace buildings. These included a great hall (long since demolished) where feasts were held. As at Westminster Hall, the King or his royal justices tried cases in the hall, and in troubled years — such as 1261 — it was used for a meeting of Parliament. The rooms, galleries and greens adjacent to it must have afforded the court considerably more comfort. From his new bedroom and privy closet in the Lanthorn Tower the King could look out upon the private garden of the palace.

Both Edward II and Edward III lived in this pleasant and secure palace. But after the latter embarked upon his foreign wars the Tower came to be seen more as a fortress to protect the city then as a royal palace: great preparations for a siege were made in 1337 when Edward III appears to have expected a French invasion. In November 1341, the King suddenly returned to England and, landing at midnight at the Tower steps, found the place insufficiently guarded, placed the governor under arrest and directed his son Edward, the Black Prince, to live in the Tower and maintain it safely.

As a boy, Richard II rode out from the Tower to meet the leaders of the Peasants' Revolt at Mile End in June 1381. While the sixteen-year-old King — son of the Black Prince — was promising to free them so that they 'be never named or held for serfs' a band of several hundreds of rebels, under Wat Tyler himself, discovered that the drawbridge of the Tower was down and the portcullis up. They burst into the Tower and proceeded to lynch the King's Chancellor and chief minister Simon Sudbury, Archbishop of Canterbury, whom they found in St John's Chapel, as well as his Treasurer and a Franciscan friar. Some of the mob entered the King's Privy Chamber and 'played the wantons, in sitting, lying and sporting them on the King's bed. And that which is more saucily, invited the King's mother to kiss with them.' Within a day or so, at a conference in Smithfield, the Mayor of London struck down Wat Tyler and the rebellion began to crumble.

Eighteen years later, years which had belied the early promise of the Black Prince's son, Richard II sealed his abdication at the Tower. At a formal ceremony in Westminster Hall the empty throne was successfully claimed by Henry Bolingbroke, the first of the Lancastrians. Shakespeare makes Richard's queen say:

> *… this is the way*
> *To Julius Caesar's ill-erected Tower,*
> *To whose flint bosom my condemned lord*
> *Is doomed a prisoner by proud Bolingbroke.*

He came once more to the Tower. After his mysterious death at the age of thirty-four in Pontefract Castle, they brought his corpse to rest a single night in the Tower, probably before the altar of St John's Chapel, before being buried in Westminster Abbey.

It was during the Wars of the Roses, primarily a dynastic conflict between the Houses of Lancaster and York, that the Tower acquired an especially bloody reputation. The feebleminded Henry VI was brought to the Tower in 1464 as a prisoner, where he remained for five years. Subsequently he met his death there, probably by a Yorkist assassin.

Edward IV had come from Sheen to the Tower in 1461 for his hurried coronation, and there entertained the most powerful of the Yorkists. On the eve of the ceremony the King dubbed thirty-two of his supporters Knights of the Bath, 'who, being arrayed in blue gowns with hoods and tokens of white silk upon their shoulders, rode before him to Westminster'.

These knights would soon see action in the battles of the Yorkist usurper against his Lancastrian rivals. The initial practice of creating Knights of the Bath is attributed to the first king of the rival House of Lancaster. As the name of the order implies, the young noblemen so honoured took part in a ritual of initiation which reflected the high ideals of chivalrous knighthood. Three knights escorted each one to a specially prepared bath on the night of the sovereign's residence, accompanied by squires singing and dancing. Then they conducted their man to St John's Chapel, where he kept his vigil until dawn. In the royal apartments a little later the King himself girded the sword upon the young man, who then went up again to the chapel to swear his oath and offer up his sword at the altar.

After a new Knight of the Bath left the chapel he found the royal master-cook standing in his path. 'I, the king's master-cook, am come to receive your spurs as my fee, and if you do anything contrary to the order of knighthood, which God forbid, I shall hack your spurs from your heels.' With this warning in his ears the knight went into the hall to watch the King eat a meal, though he himself was not allowed 'to eat nor drink at the table, nor spit, nor look about him, more than a bride'. Arraying himself in his robes, he then rode in the royal procession from the Tower to Westminster.

In the Council Chamber, some months after the death of Edward IV in 1483, his brother Richard, Duke of Gloucester, accused the powerful Lord Hastings of treason. The Duke's guards rushed into the chamber and pulled Hastings outside to Tower Green where he was promptly beheaded. This coup paved the way for the coronation of Gloucester as King Richard III. It is likely that, when Protector, Richard had already confined his nephews, the two young sons of Edward IV, to the Tower. Dominic Mancini, who was in London at the time, relates that the princes 'day by day began to be seen more rarely behind the bars and windows' until these appearances mysteriously ceased altogether. According to legend, they were smothered in their beds in the Bloody Tower. Centuries later, in Charles II's day, the bones of two boys aged ten and twelve were found buried at the foot of the steps leading up to the first floor entrance of the White Tower. Believed to be the remains of the princes, they were solemnly reinterred in Westminster Abbey.

Richard himself was slain at the Battle of Bosworth in 1485, and his body, naked except for a covering of blood and mire, was slung over the back of a horse behind his own herald and taken to Leicester for burial.

To his successor, the first Tudor king, the Tower may have seemed a place of ill omen, for his wife, Elizabeth of York, died there in childbirth. But Elizabeth's son, Henry VIII, set about improving the royal palace in the Tower. After the fire which damaged much of Westminster Palace in 1512 he built more rooms near the White Tower and on several occasions lived in the royal suite of rooms in the Lanthorn Tower. Later he added the half-timbered King's House, which stands today in the south-west corner of the inner bailey. On Oliver Cromwell's orders the palace buildings south of the White Tower were all dismantled, and only the King's House survives, serving today as the residence of the Lieutenant of the Tower.

Before that house was completed Henry had acquired Whitehall and Hampton Court from Cardinal Wolsey, so his interest in the Tower as a potential residence waned. In 1536 Anne Boleyn was taken there by water from Greenwich under suspicion of adultery and incest. She entered the fortress through the Traitor's Gate and her trial took place in the palace hall in the shadow of the White Tower. She was beheaded, by the skilled Calais swordsman whom she had wanted to perform the task, three weeks after her arrival — the first queen of England to suffer that fate. King Henry was out hunting on the day, and looked up when he heard the guns firing in the distance to announce her death. Next day he married Jane Seymour.

For all his marriages Henry produced only one legitimate son, who became Edward VI. When the approaching death of the boy-king became apparent in 1553, the Duke of Northumberland schemed so that the Protestant Lady Jane Grey should inherit the throne, rather than the rightful heir, Mary, an avowed Catholic. He married his son, Lord Guildford Dudley, to Jane and induced Edward VI to alter the succession in her favour. On the young King's death Lady Jane was proclaimed queen and on 10 July 1553 she made her public entry into the Tower as queen of England. But before she could proceed thence in the traditional manner to Westminster for her coronation she had been replaced by Mary, who had stayed in the Tower until her brother's funeral. Consequently, it was Mary who set out on Thursday 1 October to Westminster for her coronation ceremony. In the city she was greeted by 'goodly pageants, and devices therein, with music and eloquent speeches. The Queen was carried in a litter, and the Lady Elizabeth and the Lady Anne [of Cleves] followed in a chariot.'

In the following month Lady Jane Grey and her husband were tried and found guilty of high treason. Fluent in Hebrew, Greek and Latin, Lady Jane was learned as well as beautiful. She was only sixteen as she awaited death for six months with a fortitude which stemmed from her Protestant piety and purity of conscience. After the rising of Sir Thomas Wyatt, in which Jane's father, the Marquis of Dorset, had foolishly implicated himself, Queen Mary signed her death warrant. On 12 February 1554 the sentence was carried out.

Before she died they made her watch from a window as her young husband was led out to the scaffold. After what must have seemed an eternity, she had to witness the return of the cart bearing his headless body, the head wrapped separately in a cloth. Then her guards escorted her to the scaffold 'upon the green against the White Tower'. She walked calmly with a book of prayers in her hand, followed by her maids who 'wonderfully wept'.

After confessing the wrong done 'against the Queen's majesty' and affirming her personal innocence to the silent crowd, she declared her faith to them and concluded by saying: 'Good people, I pray you, so long as I am alive, to pray for me.' Having spoken a psalm in English, she turned to make herself ready for the ordeal. She gave her gloves and handkerchief to Mistress Tilney, her waiting maid, and the prayerbook to the brother of the Lieutenant of the Tower. Her outer garment, with its high standing collar, was next removed by her ladies and they gave her a linen cloth to bind about her eyes. 'I pray you despatch me quickly,' she said to the headsman, as she kneeled down in the straw. 'Will you take it off me before I lay me down?' she added, nervously. 'No,' he replied. She tied the cloth, and then groped for the block. 'What shall I do? Where is it?' A bystander guided her hand and she laid her white neck on the wood. 'Lord into thy hands I commend my spirit,' she prayed before the axe fell. A kingdom was denied her, but Lady Jane Grey will always reign as a queen in the Tower.

Queen Elizabeth, having herself been imprisoned in the Tower and in real danger of following Lady Jane Grey to the executioner's block, showed an understandable lack of desire to live there. It fell far short of her vision of a royal palace, for she could create no illusion of majesty there, nor weave her spells upon young courtiers.

Visitors to the Tower occasionally glimpsed the prisoners who were held there. In the reign of Charles I, for example, two friends of Sir John Eliot — the champion of Parliament's liberties — requested in vain permission to see him. They did actually catch sight of Denzil Holles, another imprisoned MP. With nothing to read, Holles had whiled away the long hours by exercising with dumb-bells and whirling a top. He held them up for the visitors to see, and made 'antick signs and devoted salutations at their parting'. Sir John Eliot died in his dank stone cell without trial. Many of those convicted of treason or other capital offences were executed, either in decent privacy on Tower Green, like Anne Boleyn, or in public view on Tower Hill, like the Earl of Strafford. The long list of traitors held in the Tower begins with Ranulf Flambard, Norman Bishop of Durham and chief minister of William Rufus, and ends with Rudolf Hess, Hitler's deputy, who found himself incarcerated there in 1941 after his flight from Germany.

These human prisoners have always shared the Tower with a variety of strange beasts. At first English monarchs kept their menageries in the country. During the 12th century Henry I kept lions, leopards and lynxes in the park at Woodstock. In 1235, when the Emperor Frederick II sent his brother-in-law Henry III a present of three leopards, the King moved his whole menagerie to the Tower. Well out of range of the royal nostrils, they were lodged in the Lion Tower, by the moat near the outer gatehouse. A leopard (or lion) cub born in the Tower was nearly always named after the reigning monarch, and its death was thought to bode ill for the sovereign. But the reverse did not hold good: in Elizabeth's day the Lion Tower still contained an elderly lion called 'Edward VI'. By then the collection in the Tower mustered three lionesses, a tiger, an old wolf, a porcupine and an eagle.

In Henry III's reign sightseers could inspect a camel and an elephant, the first seen in England since Roman days. Prisoners in the Tower often complained about their animal neighbours keeping them awake at night with their roars and cries. They also objected to the sinister ravens, whose descendants still hop arrogantly around the precincts. Some relief came when the Prince Regent allowed the surviving beasts to be moved to form the nucleus of the Zoological Gardens in Regent's Park. The lion called 'William IV' could be seen there in Queen Victoria's reign.

The lions in particular gave the Tower a regal presence, for lions were kings of the animal world and fitting representatives of the monarch. Perhaps the modern equivalents are the Crown Jewels. Part of the awe they inspire is the spectacle of great wealth in the small compass of a glass showcase; they also serve as relics of kings and queens, bringing us closer to those who wore them. It is a pity that most of them are late in date, for the original Crown Jewels did not survive the Civil War and Commonwealth period. Alas, we cannot touch them as earlier visitors to the Tower were allowed to do, providing that they tipped the warder. After Colonel Blood stole them in Charles II's reign, the jewels were recovered and henceforth displayed behind iron grilles. The Crown Jewels of today are mostly worn at coronations or state occasions — not in royal palaces — and they look rather theatrical to our eyes. We should give much to see that heavy plain gold crown that William the Conqueror wore on great feast days at Westminster, Winchester or Gloucester, or the lighter gold crowns that the

Plantagenets placed upon their heads before joining their lords and prelates in the royal hall within the Tower.

Yet there are one or two jewels which do arouse a feeling of excitement. One came to light when the shrine of Edward the Confessor was opened in the 12th century. The Abbot of Westminster presented it to the reigning monarch. Known as St Edward's Sapphire, it once formed part of a ring which gleamed upon the hand of Edward the Confessor. There is also a large ruby given in about 1367 to his namesake, the Black Prince, for winning the Battle of Nájera in northern Spain. Since the reign of Charles II it has been set in front of the state crown.

Charles II, the 'Merry Monarch', was in fact the last sovereign to spend a night in the Tower, before processing the next day — the eve of his coronation — to Westminster Palace. Later he commissioned Sir Christopher Wren to restore the White Tower, which had fallen into disrepair. He probably inserted the large classical windows, facing them with stone, which we see today. The King's astronomer used the round turret on the White Tower (the other three are square) for his telescope before the establishment of the Royal Observatory at Greenwich. Whether or not the astronomer actually saw stars through the thick smog which rose from London's coal fires is not recorded.

Yet it is the Yeomen Warders in their Tudor costume that link us most firmly to the days when the Tower still saw royalty in residence. In 1585 a German visitor to England called Leopold von Wedel saw Queen Elizabeth dine: 'the Yeomen of the Guard entered, bareheaded, clothed in scarlet, with a golden rose upon their backs, bringing in at each turn a course of twenty-four dishes.'

The ancient 'ceremony of the keys' — the formal locking of the gates each night — is probably older than the House of Tudor. The Chief Yeoman Warder, armed with the keys and escorted by soldiers of the Tower guard, secures the outer Middle Tower and Byward Tower gates. Then the famous challenge takes place under the black arch of the Bloody Tower:

> *'Halt, who goes there?'*
> *'The keys.'*
> *'Whose keys?'*
> *'Queen Elizabeth's keys.'*

After receiving a salute from the whole guard, the keys are taken to the King's House for the night. The Governor has custody of the keys since the Constable of the Tower no longer lives there. Constables, who for more than a century have been distinguished soldiers, receive the gold keys at their installation from the Lord Chamberlain. For the Tower, although principally famous as a citadel and state prison, is still officially the 'Royal Palace and Fortress of the Tower of London'.

2: WINDSOR

The most romantique castle in the world

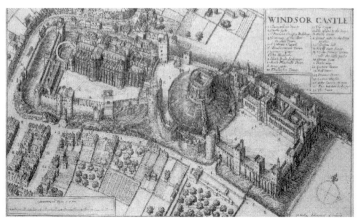

A bird's-eye view of Windsor Castle in 1658 by Wenceslas
Hollar

'Calmly from its hill-top it enjoys the most delightful view in
the world.' So wrote William Camden in the first Elizabeth's
reign. But it was the security of that hill that drew the Normans
to it, not the enchanting prospect across the far-stretching vale
patterned by ploughlands, woods and green meadows and
watered by the softly flowing Thames. William the Conqueror
built the first castle at Windsor in 1080 as a link in an iron
chain of nine fortresses, set some 20 miles apart, which
encircled his capital. Two miles downstream stood Kingsbury,
the Saxon palace at Old Windsor. Norman kings continued to
use it as a hunting lodge during the days when Windsor Castle
was no more than a round wooden keep on a 50-foot mound
in an enclosure surrounded by a stockade. But the long, narrow

13-acre bailey which stood high upon a chalk outcrop above the Thames soon held enough wooden buildings to house the court, and in 1110 Henry I kept Christmas in some state there.

His grandson Henry II, the first Plantagenet, rebuilt in stone these palace halls and apartments. To protect them he erected a new curtain wall, studded with square towers, and also replaced the wooden keep with the Round Tower, although it was much lower than the one we see today. The florid, red-haired monarch was prone to paroxysms of fury in which he would hurl himself on the floor and bite the rushes: in such a rage he indirectly ordered the death of Thomas Becket. His son John rivalled him in temper but excelled him in vindictiveness. In 1210 he threw into a Windsor dungeon the wife and son of a former favourite, Sir William de Braose, who was in Normandy trying to raise a ransom for his family. The jailers left them a sheaf of wheat and a slice of raw bacon. When the cell door was opened eleven days later King John's men saw a horrible sight: in her dying starvation agonies the mother had gnawed the cheeks of her dead son.

For such crimes and many lesser malpractices King John was compelled to sign Magna Carta in 1215 by the barons who assembled at Runnymede meadow near the castle. The following year the attempt by John to escape its stern demands brought upon Windsor Castle a major siege: for three months the Constable, with sixty knights to stiffen his garrison, successfully withstood the onslaughts of a baronial army equipped with great stone-throwing siege engines. When peace returned, John's son Henry III did much to repair the damage to Windsor Castle. Moreover, he employed some fresh ideas about fortification brought home by the Crusaders and built three new rounded towers along the western section, now flanked by the main street of Windsor.

Henry also enlarged and restored the royal hall and apartments against the north flank of the Lower Ward (the castle comprised three divisions — the Upper, Middle and Lower Wards). He added to them the largest chapel in the castle, which he dedicated to St Edward the Confessor. A fire in 1296 destroyed most of this range of palace buildings, but some medieval wall paintings survive in a house against the north wall in what may have once been Henry's bedroom.

Edward III was born in Windsor Castle in 1312 and until his accession his future subjects knew him as Edward of Windsor. It was an appropriate name, since he loved the palace and did more than any other monarch to ensure its lasting fame. Upon his orders, William of Wykeham built a handsome range of buildings round a quadrangle in the Upper Ward. In appearance they must have resembled his later collegiate foundations at Winchester and Oxford. Although these medieval halls and staircases have long since disappeared, the influence of William of Wykeham lingers on today: the state rooms and private royal apartments of later times still stand around that quadrangle. Like the castle walls, these palace buildings erected by Edward III were fashioned in silver-grey stone quarried not far away on the heathlands near Bagshot. To provide timber for roofing and flooring the new palace, the royal workmen felled a great number of oaks in Windsor Forest. In 1365 alone they axed and sawed 600 trees. According to one contemporary chronicler, 'almost all the masons and carpenters throughout the whole of England' were employed in the castle.

Edward III was a warrior-king. He was also seized with the imaginative ideals of chivalry. At the centre of this tangle of myths, legends and romances lay the shadowy ideal of the perfect Christian knight, one who was brave, true and courteous. It was supposed that a golden age of chivalry had once flourished under King Arthur. Indeed, according to the chronicler Froissart, Arthur had founded Windsor Castle and established his noble Round Table there, 'from whence so many gallant knights had issued forth and displayed the valiant prowess of their deeds at arms over the world'.

In January 1344, after much feasting and jousting, the King, then thirty-one years old, took a solemn oath that he would form a Round Table of 300 knights in the same manner as Arthur. Work began on a large circular banqueting hall to house the new Round Table, but the war in France distracted Edward's attention and the project was temporarily dropped. Fortunately, the actual Round Table built for Edward III has survived and hangs today upon a wall in Winchester Castle.

Four years later, Edward III founded a select order of chivalry, but not with the Round Table as its theme. According to one version of the story Joan, 'the Fair Maid of Kent', lost her blue garter during a dance held at court in 1347 to celebrate the fall of Calais. While the company jested at the spectacle of her discomfort, the King stepped forward, picked up the garter and tied it round his own leg, declaring '*Honi soit qui mal y pense*' — 'Shame be to him who thinks evil of it.' Gazing at the court, he added: 'You make but small account of this garter, but within a few months I will cause the best of you all to reverence the like.' Thus began the history of 'the Most Noble and Amiable Company of St George, named the Garter', comprised initially of Edward, as the Sovereign of the Order, with his son the Black Prince and twenty-four knights as the Companions.

Henry III's chapel in the Lower Ward, much restored and with its dedication enlarged to include St George and the Blessed Virgin Mary, became the centrepiece of the new

College of St George. The old royal apartments, spoilt by the fire fifty years earlier, were demolished and new houses erected for the 'spiritual' members of the foundation — the Dean and Canons of Windsor, supported by some clerks, choristers and 'Poor Knights' (veterans of gentle birth but modest means who would represent the Companions at the daily services) — whose function was to offer worship in the chapel and to pray for the souls of members of the order, living and departed. The successors of the Poor Knights, now called the Military Knights of Windsor and dressed in scarlet coats, still muster for Sunday service in St George's Chapel. A special prayer on behalf of the Most Noble Order of the Garter is daily chanted in the same place, a tradition over 600 years old.

However, the old chapel in the Lower Ward fell far short of the splendour appropriate to such an order. By 1390, when Geoffrey Chaucer was for a brief time Clerk of the King's Work at Windsor, the chapel had become ruinous, and he received orders to restore it.

The victorious Yorkist soldier who became Edward IV began the building of the present chapel, but work on it continued well into the reign of Henry VIII. With its soaring pillars and delicate veins of fan-vaulting, the walls set with stained glass of great beauty, St George's Chapel is today the most glorious building in any royal palace. If that glory came to fruition in time to be stamped with the rose, portcullis and other badges of the Tudors, yet their Yorkist predecessor must be given the full credit for conceiving it.

'Methink I am in a prison,' wrote young Edward VI at Windsor. 'Here be no galleries nor gardens to walk in.' His father Henry VIII, whose body lay buried in St George's Chapel, had rebuilt the main gateway (which now bears his name) but had saved his money for other palaces. Edward's half-sister Elizabeth made a gallery between a three-storeyed building with oriel windows (named after her grandfather Henry VII, who had caused it to be built) and the gate to the Upper Ward. Much restored, these two structures now form part of the present Royal Library and can still be seen today.

Elizabeth also enlarged and extended the North Terrace with a covered walk on top of it, giving her courtiers wide views over the Thames valley. Below the terrace her gardeners created a new garden 'full of meanders and labyrinths'. Although Elizabeth found the castle very cold in winter she appreciated the 'deliciousness' of the site. She could be seen walking briskly on the broad terrace 'to catch her a heat in the mornings'. Probably in 1602 the Queen saw there the first performance of Shakespeare's *The Merry Wives of Windsor*. It had been written at her express command 'in a fortnight'. It is just possible that the 14th-century hall of the minor canons in the Lower Ward, which subsequently became the Chapter Library, served as the theatre upon that occasion. It is said that the Queen was 'very well pleased at the representation'.

At the beginning of the Civil War a garrison from Parliament's army occupied Windsor Castle. Thus Prince Rupert found the gates closed in his face when he surrounded the castle during the advance of his uncle Charles I and the main Royalist army on London in the autumn of 1642. The Royalist train of artillery bombarded the walls for seven hours, but the Cavaliers could make no impression on the resolve of the garrison. During the war that followed the castle served as a prison for captured Royalist officers.

At a great three-day prayer meeting in St George's Chapel, held on the eve of the Second Civil War of 1648, Cromwell and his captains determined 'to call Charles Stuart, that man of blood' to account. After his execution, not twelve months later, the headless body of the King was laid first in his bedchamber and then in St George's Hall before being buried under the floor of the chapel. As they carried him to rest, the cold February day clouded over and the snowflakes fell thick and fast: 'by the time the corpse had reached the west end of the Chapel, the black pall was white'.

After the death of Charles I, the castle was again garrisoned by soldiers of Parliament. Former generals of Parliament such as Sir William Waller and Sir Richard Browne, who found themselves at odds with the dictatorship of the army, now occupied the prison rooms vacated by the Royalists. Cromwell occasionally resided at Windsor Castle and did his best to maintain the palace buildings and their contents. He ensured that regular services were held in St George's Chapel and revived the foundation of Poor Knights. As a mark of their gratitude several of these old soldiers, though Royalist to a man, struggled to London to attend Cromwell's funeral.

King Charles II appointed as his second Constable of Windsor Castle the illustrious Prince Rupert. When the diarist John Evelyn visited the castle in 1670 he found it 'exceedingly ragged and ruinous', the old rooms being 'melancholy and of ancient magnificence'. Prince Rupert, he reported, had begun 'to trim up the keep, or high round tower'. By his orders, martial displays of pikes and muskets now festooned the walls of the steep staircase leading up to it. Leaving such military displays to his uncle, the King had meanwhile completed his plans for transforming the palace buildings in the Upper Ward.

Working under the direction of the royal architect Hugh May, workmen constructed St George's Hall (destroyed in 1826) and Star Building on the site of the old Plantagenet apartments fronting the North Terrace. Although unimposing from the outside, the interiors conveyed something of the grandeur of Versailles. The hall is said to have inspired Wren (who was son of a Dean of Windsor) to model the Painted Hall at Greenwich upon it. Antonio Verrio, then Court Painter, covered the walls and ceiling with allegorical messages about royalty, including one scene depicting Charles II in the company of Fortitude, Prudence and Temperance. The carvings of Grinling Gibbons and rich tapestries and paintings made the buildings truly palatial. Nor did Charles neglect to improve the setting. In order to go out and return from hunting in style he decreed that the Long Walk should be made, a magnificent avenue of elms stretching away from Star Building to a low hill in Windsor Great Park some 3 miles away.

Charles II enjoyed living in Windsor Castle and usually contrived to spend the late summer there, for September was the best month for hunting. He fished in the Thames at Datchet, sculled upon its waters and hawked along the riverbanks and hedgerows. He indulged a passion by attending horse races on the flats opposite Datchet, west of the castle. He played tennis on a court he had built there and took his dogs for long walks in the Park. For his mistress Nell Gwyn he built a house outside the walls, reputedly connected to the state apartments by an underground tunnel. Later this house passed to her son by him, the Duke of St Albans.

Queen Anne also liked hunting and spent much time at Windsor. One of the 'rides' or avenues in the Great Park bears her name, doubtless commemorating those days when — too corpulent to ride safely — the elderly sovereign mounted a horse-drawn chariot in order to follow her beloved staghounds. She lived not in the castle itself but in a 'small neat house' just outside it.

The first two Georges did not care for Windsor. But in 1776 George III gave Anne's house to his queen. 'This will give us the means of some pleasant jaunts to that beautiful park,' wrote the King to Lord North. The following year the Queen paid the Duke of St Albans £4,000 for his mother Nell Gwyn's old house. This building, some 200 yards down the hill, became known as the Lower Lodge, to distinguish it from the Upper or Queen's Lodge. As George's family grew in number, Sir William Chambers extended the Queen's Lodge eastwards until it formed a barrack-like building parallel to the south wall of the castle and only 40 yards away from it.

'Our habitation is just the thing for us,' wrote Queen Charlotte to her midshipman son. Every summer now saw the royal family at Windsor. George III immersed himself there in the life of a country squire. Charles Knight, son of a local bookseller, recalled in his memoirs: 'The park was a glory for cricket and kite-flying. The King would stand alone to see the boys at cricket. He was a quiet, good-humoured gentleman in a long blue coat; and many a time had he bidden us good morning when we were hunting for mushrooms in the early dew and he was returning from his dairy to his eight o'clock breakfast. Everyone knew that most respectable and amiable of country squires and His Majesty knew everyone.'

In 1789 the King, after recovering from his first bout of madness (when he was confined in a straitjacket at Kew), returned to Windsor. He expressed his feelings for the place by wearing his Windsor uniform of 'blue and gold turned up with red', which he had had designed in 1778. The royal family spent their evenings together, the children writing or reading at a large table or listening to music — usually by Handel, their father's favourite composer. On warm evenings they walked on the terrace, greeting the crowd who thronged it to watch the promenade.

By 1804 James Wyatt, the King's young Surveyor-General, had restored much of the castle in the medieval Gothic style and George III moved into the Upper Ward from the Queen's Lodge. Here, in the north front rooms, George III lingered during the last ten years of his life, victim of intermittent mental illness, until he died there in 1820. The Prince Regent, now George IV, resolved to create at Windsor a palace fit for his expensive — rather than exalted — vision of royalty. He commissioned Jeffrey Wyatt, nephew of James, who petitioned the King to allow him to change his name to Wyatville to avoid confusion with his uncle. 'Veal or mutton, call yourself what you like,' replied George, putting the pretensions of the man into perspective.

At a cost of more than a million pounds, Wyatville created the palace more or less as we see it today. The new private apartments on the sunny east and south sides of the quadrangle were raised by the height of an extra storey to provide servants' rooms and were refashioned in the battlemented Gothic style, as were the buildings of Charles II on the North Terrace which housed the state apartments. He added the Banqueting Rooms and Grand Corridor to link up the three fronts.

Wyatville also raised the Round Tower by 30 feet to its present height, which was a touch of genius. Then he brought the Long Walk right up to the George IV Gate in the quadrangle itself, thus completing that grand avenue flanked by double rows of elms. The Queen's Lodge, which had stood in the way and was too uncomfortably near the town prison for George's liking, had been demolished several years earlier.

After the defeat of Napoleon at Waterloo on 18 June 1815, Sir Thomas Lawrence was commissioned to paint the portraits of the allied leaders who had encompassed the downfall of the tyrant. In order to provide a suitable gallery for this series a competition was held which Wyatville won. By his plan the old Horn Court was roofed over and made into the Waterloo Chamber. Since 1914 the Waterloo Day banquet has been held annually in this room, save for the interruptions of less gentlemanly wars.

George must have annoyed the Duke of Wellington on occasions. His father had repeatedly refused his request as a young man to be allowed to join the army and instead George soldiered entirely in his fertile imagination. His grasp of the distinction between fact and fiction often became shaky, especially after several glasses of brandy. He once recounted some spectacular adventures whereby he had virtually saved the day at the Battle of Salamanca — to the Duke of Wellington of all people! Yet Wellington summed up his sovereign as 'the most extraordinary compound of talent, wit, buffoonery, obstinacy and good feeling — in short a medley of the most opposite qualities, with a greater preponderance of good — that I ever saw in any character in my life'.

After Queen Victoria's marriage, Prince Albert converted her to the joys of country life: coming to Windsor from London came to feel like being 'freed from some dungeon'. But in comparison to her other homes even Windsor seemed 'prison-like'. Writing to her daughter Vicky in 1858, she observed: 'I have never felt Windsor more dull or tiresome — or the Castle stiffer and gloomier than this year! I long for our cheerful and unpalacelike rooms at Osborne and Balmoral.'

Yet Victoria herself contributed to this boring and formal atmosphere over the years. It was relieved only by petty domestic scandals and the usual gossip. Even the grand state visits of foreign crowned heads became something of a routine. The renovated Curfew Tower is a monument to one such visit. The royal architects modelled it upon the towers of Carcassonne, which Napoleon III was in the process of restoring when he was the Queen's guest at Windsor in 1855. For the occasion the Waterloo Chamber was tactfully renamed the Picture Gallery.

The 'noxious effluvia' which arose from the medieval drainage system and numerous cesspools of Windsor Castle may have helped to cause the typhoid which killed Prince Albert in 1861. The Queen commemorated 'this dreadful day' by creating the Albert Memorial Chapel, but still more she attempted to make the castle a shrine to her husband's memory. A servant placed hot water and a freshly pressed suit of clothes in Albert's room every day. Even the glass from which he had last drunk medicine remained on his bedside table for forty years. Still to be seen are the railings of the walk on the roof of the Dean's Cloister, which the 'Widow of Windsor' had made so that she could pass from the Deanery into St George's Chapel without being observed by her subjects. In the chapel she sat behind that same stone grille, high on the north side of the altar, where Catherine of Aragon had once knelt to observe the mass being celebrated below her.

From this vantage point Victoria witnessed the marriage of her son, the future Edward VII. We can only speculate upon what her thoughts would have been had she lived to hear the Abdication broadcast of that King's grandson, Edward VIII. Not long after his accession the popular young King forfeited his throne for the sake of Mrs Wallis Simpson, an American who had been married twice before. For Edward VIII paradise on earth could not be found in palaces without the support of the woman he loved. Years later the body of the Duke of Windsor was brought back for burial in Windsor Castle.

Today the greater part of Windsor Castle is open to the general public and hosts of tourists come from overseas, but it remains very much a palace. Indeed, it is the only English royal residence of the present day that has been in continuous use since the early Middle Ages. The Queen's private apartments overlooking the south and east terraces provide a sanctuary for her and her family at weekends and during more extended periods of residence, notably Ascot Week, so that despite the tourist throngs there are still moments inside Windsor Castle which give that experience of royalty which the builders of palaces sought to capture and convey for their masters. There are moments of pageantry which evoke the extraordinary continuity of kingship in England. Great works of art, such as the collection of Leonardo da Vinci's drawings, are fitting treasures for such a palace.

Seen from afar Windsor Castle is a delight to the eye. The best place from which to view it is the road that runs through Windsor Great Park from Bagshot. John Milton, who lived for a time at nearby Horton, had such a summer vision as greets us there when he penned the words:

> *Towers and battlements he sees,*
> *Bosomed high in tufted trees.*

As Samuel Pepys declared on seeing Windsor Castle for the first time in 1665: 'It is the most romantique castle in the world.'

3: HAMPTON COURT

More like unto a paradise than any earthly habitation

The ceiling of the Great Hall of Hampton Court Palace

In 1514 Thomas Wolsey leased a manor from the Knights Hospitallers beside the Thames and opposite the small town of Kingston. Here he built for himself a great house which he called Hampton Court. Around six courts stood a palace of a thousand rooms. Turrets, towers and chimneys 'stretching to the stars' rose above acres of leaded roofs. Wolsey could doubtless justify the enormous cost of 200,000 gold crowns, many millions in modern money, by stressing the need for Henry VIII's first minister to be able to impress foreign ambassadors with England's affluence. Impressed they certainly were! 'One has to traverse eight rooms before one reaches his audience chamber,' reported Sebastian Giustiniani, the Venetian ambassador, not without admiration, 'and they are all hung with tapestry which is changed every week.' Wolsey loved rich and costly tapestries.

In 1525 he took the prudent step of giving Hampton Court and its priceless contents to the King, who allowed him to live there until his fall from favour four years later. The Flemish ambassador, telling the Regent of the Netherlands about the gift, added tartly: 'It seems to me that this is as good as if he had said, "I give you a little pig of your own breeding at your own great cost."'

After Wolsey's death Henry found much to admire in his new palace: the tapestries vividly depicting scenes from the Bible, classical mythology and romance; the countless Eastern carpets; and the profusion of gold, silver and gilt plates and ornaments. He may also have appreciated the freshness of the water that flowed from Wolsey's private pipeline. For Wolsey connected the palace with the pure water springs of Coombe Hill, 3 miles away, by means of lead pipes which ran under the Thames.

But like any new house-owner the King determined upon several alterations. The emblems of Wolsey were replaced by royal badges, although Wolsey's coat-of-arms in terracotta survived upon the inner gatehouse between the two main courts that is known today as Anne Boleyn's Gateway. Meanwhile, Henry's builders began work on a new gallery, library and state apartments: the first floor for Henry, with

Queen Catherine of Aragon above him and their daughter Mary below them on the ground floor. Elsewhere in the palace, servants prepared lodgings for the King's 'entirely beloved sweetheart', Anne Boleyn. To show off before the ladies his martial and sporting skills, the King built a tiltyard, archery butts, tennis court and bowling alley.

The King replaced Wolsey's hall with a new great hall, containing a fine carved hammer-beam roof and musicians' gallery. Other improvements included enlargements to the kitchens, wine and beer cellars and adjacent rooms, such as the bakehouse, pantry, larder, pastry and poultry. Here a hundred or more retainers worked under the generalship of the master-cook — a magnificent figure in velvet and satin with a gold chain about his neck — to load the royal table with a profusion of meats and confectionery. As for drink, a duke or duchess had a personal allowance of 3 gallons of ale and a pitcher of wine daily, while groom porters, yeomen and others received a gallon of ale at each meal. Such expense alarmed Thomas Cromwell, Wolsey's successor as chief minister. With his eyes more upon his account books than the glory of King Henry as a Renaissance monarch, he observed: 'What a great charge it is to the King to continue his buildings in so many places at once. How proud and false the workmen be; and if the King would spare for one year how profitable it would be to him.'

After Anne Boleyn's execution Henry married Jane Seymour, who died shortly after giving birth to Edward, his only legitimate son. For political reasons he married next Anne of Cleves, whom he disposed of by divorce. His fifth wife, Catherine Howard, has most associations with Hampton Court. She was a light-hearted and lively young girl, rather plump and less than 5 feet in height, with reddish hair and hazel eyes. To Henry she seemed a wonderful wife; he called her 'a rose without a thorn' and his 'jewel of womanhood'.

While Henry was attending mass in the chapel, praying under the new and magnificent wooden fan-vaulted ceiling, Archbishop Cranmer passed him a note from the Privy Council with information that his bride of little more than a year had been unfaithful to him. Henry 'so tenderly loved the woman' and trusted her so completely that at first he suspected a forgery. At the Council Chamber he was shown the proofs, which left him dumb in heavy thought for several minutes. Then he wept as he uttered 'the sorrow of his heart unto us'. His love and sorrow, however, would soon turn to hatred and rage.

The Queen was brought to trial at Hampton Court and the story of her misdemeanours became more widely known. During her cross-examination Catherine admitted a childish passion for her music-teacher, Henry Mannox, and an early affair with Francis Dereham, one of the retainers of her uncle, the Duke of Norfolk, whom she took into her service after she became queen. When Catherine married the ailing, middle-aged King in 1540 she was still only about twenty years old and she soon found the temptations of court life irresistible. The flattery and flirtations of several courtiers, notably her cousin, Thomas Culpeper, a gentleman of the Privy Chamber, overcame her common sense. Dereham had certainly entered her chambers fairly often and 'very lewdly' during the royal northern tour of that year. Adultery itself is never easy to prove; the Queen would only admit:

> As for carnal knowledge, I confess as I did before, that divers times he has lain with me, sometimes in his doublet and hose, and two or three times naked: but not so naked that he had nothing upon him; for he had

always at the least his doublet, and as I do think, his hose also: but I mean, naked, when his hose was put down.

Yet the intention of adultery by or with the Queen was a treasonable offence. Culpeper and Dereham were put to death at Tyburn. Culpeper, nobly born, had the privilege of being beheaded; Dereham suffered the barbarities of being hanged, drawn and quartered. Catherine and her accomplice, Lady Rochford, paid their penalty on Tower Green on the eve of St Valentine's Day in 1542.

On Sunday, the day before her execution, she had asked for the block to be brought to her so that she might rehearse. At the scaffold Catherine revealed by her speech a young woman grown wise beyond her twenty or so summers.

Brothers [she said], *by the journey upon which I am bound I have not wronged the King, but it is true, that long before the King took me, I loved Culpeper, and I wish to God I had done as he wished me, for at the time the King wanted to take me, he urged me to say that I was pledged to him. If I had done as he advised me, I should not die the death, nor would he. I would rather have him for husband than be mistress of the world. But sin blinded me, and greed of grandeur, and since mine is the fault, mine also is the suffering and my great sorrow is that Culpeper should have to die through me.*

Her last words, before she knelt in prayer, summed up her short life and serve as her epitaph: 'I die a queen but I would rather die the wife of Culpeper.'

There have been those who have claimed to see the screaming ghost of Catherine, running down the haunted gallery in Hampton Court with a 'ghastly look of despair' upon her face. According to legend, she once tried to reach Henry while he was at mass in the chapel to plead with him. The royal attendants caught her in the gallery and carried her sobbing back to her apartments. Be that as it may, Hampton Court has cause to remember Catherine Howard above all Henry's 'ill-conditioned wives', as he called them in the mood of morose self-pity which settled upon him after her infidelity was disclosed. Architects may build noble palaces, but unpredictable human nature rarely makes life inside them quite the paradise which kings intend.

Henry's daughter, Mary, brought her husband, King Philip of Spain, to Hampton Court for their honeymoon, perhaps the happiest weeks in her life. In 1554 a nursery was set up in the palace, but news of Mary's pregnancy proved to be false and she died childless.

Queen Elizabeth also liked Hampton Court and, as her father and sister had done, sought to impress all with a strong sense of her majesty. In a gorgeously arrayed court she always saw to it that she was the centrepiece. Wearing one of her 3,000 dresses and a selection of her beloved jewels, she epitomized the wealth and grandeur of the Tudor dynasty at its height. During her father's reign, 'Your Highness', the traditional way of addressing the sovereign, gave place to 'Your Majesty'. In all that she did or said Elizabeth was intent upon being 'Her Majesty': her palaces reflected this new sense of glory.

If Elizabeth listened to the flatterers — courtiers, poets and painters — who elevated her to the status of a semi-divine goddess, a perpetual virgin dedicated to her high calling, Hampton Court proved to be a suitably ethereal palace for her to act out that fantasy. The foreign visitor, Paul Hentzner, described it in glowing terms: 'In short, all the walls of the palace shine with gold and silver. Here is also a certain cabinet [room] called Paradise where besides that everything glitters so with silver, gold and jewels, as to dazzle one's eyes, there is a musical instrument made all of glass except the strings.' Even the tapestries in the Paradise Chamber gleamed with pearls. Diamonds shone in the ceiling. A canopied throne covered with brown velvet threaded with gold and set with gems stood in the room. Beneath the canopy 'the Queen is accustomed to sit in her magnificence, upon a very stately chair covered with cushions'.

Music, the language of glory, always played an important part in creating the experience of living a more than human life in a palace. Trumpets sounded at the grand set-piece ceremonies. Through open windows visitors could hear Elizabeth's ladies playing upon their instruments. Sir James Melville, the envoy of Mary, Queen of Scots, was once taken to the room where Elizabeth herself was playing the virginals (an early form of harpsichord) in order to satisfy the Queen's curiosity as to whether she or Mary was the better musician. She pretended to be surprised when she saw him, and 'came forward, seeming to strike me with her hand, alleging that she used not to play before men, but when she was solitary to shun melancholy'.

In 1604 James I summoned a great conference in the King's Privy Chamber at Hampton Court. The bishops of the Church of England were to meet with their Puritan critics and reach agreement on the form of religion to be recognized in the kingdom. The idea behind it was a good one: the King as head of the Church of England would be seen to restore peace and harmony by arbitrating between the theological factions. But the reality fell far short of the idea. The King talked mostly in Latin and at great length, disputing with the Puritan champions, though he resorted more to upbraidings than arguments. 'I have peppered them soundly,' he informed a friend in Scotland by letter. He 'told them they wanted to strip Christ again and bid them away with their snivelling. Moreover, he wished those who would take away the surplice might want linen for their own breech!' One pleased bishop declared that His Majesty spoke by the power of inspiration: if so, commented Sir John Harington, 'the spirit was rather foul-mouthed'.

Perhaps the bishops and divines took a turn round the royal gardens which, in Elizabeth's day, contained a profusion of cherry, apple and pear trees. In her father's time the whole garden was divided into squares, quartered into lawns and ponds and ablaze with flowers. The paths were lined with painted heraldic beasts on pillars and fenced with 960 yards of railings painted in the Tudor colours of white and green. In the reign of Charles I distinctly untheological thoughts were to occupy the Cavalier poet, Sir John Suckling, as he trod those paths. In a poem *Upon my Lady Carlisle's walking in Hampton Court Garden*, he and Thomas Carew slowly stripped that lady naked in their imaginations:

> *I was undoing all she wore,*
> *And had she walked but one turn more,*
> *Eve in her first state had not been*
> *More naked, or more plainly seen.*

A masterpiece was born at the Hampton Court Conference — the Authorised Version or King James's Bible. But that indissoluble unity 'twixt monarchy and episcopacy, which James declared to be an article of faith to the Puritans — 'No bishop, no king!' — helped to lead one day to his son Charles I being brought a close prisoner of a victorious Parliament to Hampton Court. There Cromwell talked with the royal captive several times, seeking to find some formula for a constitutional settlement. The impassive Charles played his cards so close to his chest that even he never quite realized that he no longer held any aces.

After two months the King determined to escape from Hampton Court. On the night of 11 November 1647 he left the palace with Colonel Legge, passing through the Paradise Chamber and by various private passages to the riverside, where two loyal followers met him with horses. Colonel Whalley, who had been left in charge of the King, gradually became suspicious as no sounds came from the locked royal bedchamber. Eventually, guided by the Keeper of the Privy Lodgings to another door, Whalley strode 'from chamber to chamber till we came to the next chamber to his Majesty's bedchamber, where we saw his Majesty's cloak lying on the midst of the floor, which much amazed me.' The King made his way to Carisbrooke Castle on the Isle of Wight, where he continued along that path of duplicity which would lead to the Second Civil War and the axe at Whitehall.

Republicans such as Sir Henry Vane, a former Governor of New England, favoured dismantling Hampton Court for, he said, 'it was among those things that prove temptations to ambitious men and exceedingly tend to sharpen their appetite to ascend the throne'. (What he would have thought of the White House in Washington we can only surmise.) Various items, such as Cardinal Wolsey's looking-glass and Henry VIII's walking stick, were sold at auction (for £5 and 5 shillings respectively), but the palace was kept intact.

Cromwell used Hampton Court as a country retreat and hunting lodge. The Lord Protector could be merry and mirthful on occasions, and a somewhat hostile Royalist writer pictures him at the weekly dinners for officers of the army entertaining them with 'a hundred antic tricks, as throwing of cushions and putting live coals in their pockets and boots... He had twenty other freaks in his head, for sometimes before he had half dined, he would give order for a drum to beat, and call in his Foot Guards, like a kennel of hounds, to snatch off the meat from his table and tear it in pieces.'

When, at the age of thirty-two, Charles II married Catherine of Braganza, he brought her to Hampton Court for their honeymoon. She was closely watched by some of her new subjects, who speculated whether or not she would 'put Madame Castlemaine's nose out of joint'. Her Portuguese retinue, according to one observer, contained 'six frights who called themselves maids of honour, and a duenna, another monster who took the title of governess to these extraordinary beauties'. But in the opinion of Samuel Pepys the Queen was no match for Lady Castlemaine, the King's favourite mistress of the day, who was about to have his second child.

Architecturally, Charles added little to Hampton Court beyond some landscaped gardens set with yew trees in the straight avenues that he favoured and made fashionable. William and Mary, however, once they were convinced their throne was secure, decided to make the palace one of their principal residences. Sir Christopher Wren received a commission to draw up plans and he conceived a building which would rival the Louvre: a grand classical Renaissance-style mansion in red brick and Portland stone to replace the Tudor palace. Two courts were ruthlessly pulled down and a third remodelled as work progressed over the next five years, but the Great Hall was mercifully spared. Yet it must be added that Wren's buildings — the Park Block and Privy Gate Block, which together form the east and south sides of Fountain Court — blend in well with the more ancient red brick of the parent palace.

As joint sovereigns, William and Mary expected equal treatment when it came to the state rooms. The Queen's first-floor apartments along the east side of Fountain Court matched those of the King on the south side, just as *his* staircase duplicated *her* staircase. Verrio set to work to cover the ceilings and walls with paintings on classical themes, while Grinling Gibbons and his craftsmen carved the woodwork. But the building of the palace proceeded far too slowly for the impatient monarchs, for 'want of money and Portland stone' grumbled Mary to her husband.

A French visitor in Charles II's reign had damned Hampton Court with faint praise: 'a magnificent pile of building, but, upon my word, it comes not up either to our St Germain or Fontainebleau, no more than Whitehall is to be put in the same scale with the Louvre, or St James's house with Luxembourg palace.' Keeping up with the French, that occupational disease of English palace-builders, had now produced, under William and Mary, a fine country palace of which the English were justly proud. Daniel Defoe believed that when — or rather if — it was ever finished, only Versailles would rival it. The Queen had already altered the gardens to conform to the formal French style, and built herself an orangery there. She sent one of her gardeners to America to collect rare flowers and fruits from Virginia. The great vine in Old Pond Garden, however, dates from 1769: it is one of the few changes that 'Capability' Brown permitted himself to make in the gardens, which he thought extremely tasteful.

After Mary's death William continued to reside for as long as he could at Hampton Court. But while riding in the Park there, his horse put a foot in a mole hole, tripped and threw him, an accident which eventually caused his death. The Jacobites later drank toasts to 'the little gentleman in black velvet' who had excavated the fatal hole.

George I, his successor, also found the palace a pleasant place to live, although his unpopular German mistress hardly enhanced life at Hampton Court. His son George, as Prince of Wales, and Princess Caroline — with their circle of young friends — did, however, introduce some gaiety once more when they held court there. In the mornings there were river expeditions in richly decorated barges, rowed by oarsmen in royal liveries. The Prince and Princess dined in public. In the afternoon they drank chocolate in one of the pavilions by the bowling green. Card games occupied the evenings, with an occasional dance in the Queen's Gallery.

Prince George lusted for several of the ladies in their silk and satin gowns, notably 'smiling Mary Bellenden, soft and fair as dawn'. She was avidly pursued by him, quite regardless of the fact that she was known to be in love with her husband-to-be, one of the grooms of the King's bedchamber. She had to cross her arms over her bosom to stop the Prince of Wales touching her breasts 'and told him I was not cold but I liked to stand so'. One evening the Prince came to the point by sitting and clinking gold coins beside her. 'Sir,' she cried out at last, 'I can bear it no longer; if you count your money any more I shall go out of the room.'

Some years later, when he returned as George II, that springtime of flirtations and *amours* in the palace and gardens remained only a memory. Although the morals of the King and his circle had grown no better, that note of irresponsible enjoyment so often focused upon the heir to the throne was missing. The King spent his days in hunting in the hearty German fashion. 'We hunt with great noise and violence,' wrote Mrs Howard, later Countess of Suffolk, 'and have every day a tolerable chance of having a neck broken.' As a lady of the Queen's bedchamber (though, as the royal mistress, she was fairly familiar with the King's bedchamber as well) Mrs Howard could observe the prosaic life of the Hanoverian royal family. In the evening the King usually strolled up and down holding forth about the genealogies or military affairs that interested him — he had fought with distinction at Oudenarde in 1708 and would take part in the Battle of Dettingen in 1743. The Queen, sitting at her tapestry work, 'knotted and yawned, till from yawning she came to nodding, and from nodding to snoring'. Doubtless she looked forward to the clock striking nine, when the King would check his watch and depart to Mrs Howard's rooms.

The poet Alexander Pope observed the boring life of the court at first hand. His *Rape of the Lock* had made an epic out of a minor squabble in Hampton Court during the previous reign, when Lord Petrie had ruined a dinner party by snipping a lock from Miss Arabella Fermor's hair as she bent over her cup of coffee. Mrs Howard, Mary Bellenden and Miss Lepell conversed with him one day after coming back from hunting: 'We all agreed that the life of a Maid of Honour was of all things the most miserable, and wished that every woman who envied had a specimen of it. To eat Westphalia ham in a morning, ride over hedges and ditches on borrowed hacks, come home in the heat of the day with a fever, and (what is worse a thousand times) with a red mark on the forehead from an uneasy hat.'

On one occasion George II is said to have boxed the ears of his grandson in the state rooms at Hampton Court. When that grandson came to the throne as George III in 1760 he never slept a night at Hampton Court, apparently because the palace was always associated in his mind with that unhappy memory. He took out most of the furniture and granted 'grace and favour' apartments in the palace to those who merited it.

Dr Samuel Johnson once applied to the Lord Chamberlain for one of these apartments: 'I hope, to a man who has had the honour of vindicating his Majesty's government, a retreat in one of his houses may be not improperly or unworthily allowed,' he urged. But his request was not granted. The residences were reserved for those persons or their relatives who had rendered distinguished service to Crown and country. The Countess of Mornington lived there and received visits from her son, the Duke of Wellington. He named one nook in the east front Purr Corner, because he used to see the old ladies sitting there, sleeping or chatting in the sun.

Thus Hampton Court became, in William IV's apt phrase, 'the quality poor house'.

4: WHITEHALL

'Tis now the King's and called Whitehall

The Old Palace of Whitehall by Hendrik Danckerts, c. 1675

The Palace of Whitehall began its history as 'the inn of the Archbishop of York within the Bars of Westminster', a 'low wretched building only two storeys high'. When Thomas Wolsey became Archbishop of York he at once enlarged and embellished York Place, as it was called. Even the cooks and kitchen servants of 'the proudest prelate that ever breathed' wore velvet and satin livery with gleaming chains round their necks. In the hall meals cooked and carried by these retainers were served to guests on gold and silver plates, including an entertainment in 1518 when they produced 'a sumptuous supper the like of which was never given by Cleopatra or Caligula'.

One guest who observed with keen interest both this magnificent style of living and the improvements to the already grand buildings was Wolsey's political master, Henry VIII. After fire had destroyed much of Westminster Palace in 1512 the King stood in sore need of such a London house. His opportunity came in 1529, after Wolsey as his chief minister had failed to procure the divorce from Catherine of Aragon that Henry so passionately wanted. In October that year the Cardinal again offered Henry all his possessions: next month the new owner moved into York Place. 'Sir,' says one of the gentleman at the coronation of Anne Boleyn in Shakespeare's *Henry VIII*:

> *You must no more call it York Place; that's past:*
> *For since the Cardinal fell, that title's lost;*
> *'Tis now the King's and called Whitehall.*

The whole of Wolsey's palace had been situated between the river and the thoroughfare leading from Charing Cross to Westminster. In order to construct for himself the largest palace in Christendom Henry acquired more land beyond this road and demolished hundreds of houses. On the 24-acre site he began to build the palace which would proclaim the glory of his dynasty. The dismantled Privy Gallery from Wolsey's confiscated country palace at Esher was reconstructed at Whitehall, one of a chain of interconnecting galleries and halls which gave an Italian visitor, the Count of Belgrade, this vivid impression in 1531:

> *Long porticoes or halls, without chambers, with windows on each side looking on gardens or the river, the ceilings being marvellously wrought in stone and gold, and the wainscot of carved wood representing a thousand beautiful figures; and round about there are chambers and very large halls, all hung with tapestry.*

Even in those days, however, it was impossible to ignore well established rights of way. The street, like the modern Whitehall, was a public thoroughfare and could not be closed. In effect this street bisected the palace area and destroyed any unity which the royal architects may have envisaged. West of the street lay an area enclosed by a wall wherein lay the gardens, a cockpit, a tiltyard, tennis courts, a bowling alley, 'a ball-house where they play at featherballs' (a form of badminton) and other buildings for pleasure or sport. Two gateways — the King Street and the Holbein Gates — were built astride this street to give access to the park side of the palace, or the Cockpitside as it came to be known. The Holbein Gate stood almost opposite the southern end of the present Banqueting House and the King Street Gate gave access to King Street at the south-western corner of the palace precincts.

On the river side of the road an imposing turreted gateway known as Whitehall or Palace Gate kept passers-by from straying into the Great Court of the palace. Like a rambling collection of Oxford colleges jammed together, it contained a warren of paved courts which became less grand the further one moved from the Great Court. Those inner recesses, unvisited by the King or his courtiers, were inhabited by the legions of household servants. Each court acquired a name, such as the Preaching Court, where a pulpit stood in the middle of a garden for outdoor sermons. This profusion of galleries, halls, towers and lodgings, arranged around courts of all sizes and shapes, peopled by a noisy throng of courtiers and servants, lacked any order or uniform vision. It was the architectural equivalent of the King's spreading girth. An Italian visitor in the next century, looking at Whitehall with a realistic eye, judged it to be 'nothing more than an heap of houses, badly built at different times and for different purposes'.

Yet there were glories to behold. Hans Holbein, who became Court Painter in 1536, adorned many of the ceilings and walls. He painted upon one wall in the Privy Chamber an imposing portrait of the King, flanked by his parents and his queen, Jane Seymour. It had the desired effect on some visitors, for one who saw it wrote that 'the King as he stood there, majestic in his splendour, was so lifelike that the spectator felt abashed, annihilated in his presence'. No artist before Holbein had portrayed the sovereign of England with such effect. Palaces were the architectural counterpart of such paintings, and it is fitting that the gatehouse where Holbein lodged while he worked in Whitehall Palace should have borne his name in subsequent centuries.

Henry VIII had married Anne Boleyn, already pregnant with the future Queen Elizabeth, in a turret of Whitehall. Elizabeth became fond of the palace and used it for those splendid tournaments and masques over which she loved to preside. Today Queen Elizabeth II's official birthday is celebrated by an equally splendid parade of her red-coated guardsmen in Horse Guards Parade. It takes an effort of the imagination now to picture the tiltyard which once occupied a part of the site. The first Elizabeth sat in the Tiltyard Gallery to watch knights jousting below and breaking lances across the beam at least twice a year in her honour, on her birthday and on the anniversary of her accession.

Always there were ambassadors or envoys to impress, either to win the friendship of their masters or to deter their enmity. In 1559, for example, Elizabeth held a feast to welcome the Duke of Montmorency. The great ground-floor Stone Gallery, hung with gold and silver brocade, blazed with flowers. The royal party sat at one table, the ambassadors at another and the remaining company at a third, some fifty-four paces in length. The Venetian ambassador enjoyed 'the large and excellent joints' of beef and mutton, but found the English fell short of the standards of 'delicacies and cleanliness' customary in Italy. The seating plan, if there was one, had not allowed for the width of the ladies' dresses, and some guests found themselves eating their supper sitting on the floor on the rushes. After the banquet they watched a thirteen-a-side tournament in the tiltyard, a 'theatre celestial' lit by a great number of torches held aloft by the Guard. It was a great success, for the Venetian thought it 'a sight exceeding glorious… as can hardly be seen the like in any Christian Court'.

The Stone Gallery, divided into three apartments, was clearly not suitable for such occasions and the old archiepiscopal hall was probably too small. For the visit in 1581 of one of her suitors, the Duke of Alençon, the Queen had a canvas marquee erected, about 100 yards long with a roof supported by thirty 'great masts', each 40 feet high. The walls were painted on the outside to resemble stonework, while inside the court painters daubed the canopy with the sun, clouds and stars. This 'temporary' banqueting house, made in twenty-four days, survived as many years, until 1606 when James I replaced it with a stone building. Perhaps symbolically his hall lasted a much shorter time. In 1619 some workmen clearing up after a masque lit a fire inside to burn the rubbish and within an hour the whole hall lay in smoking ruins.

Inigo Jones, the architect commissioned to rebuild it, completed the new Banqueting House in three years at a cost of over £15,000. It is the only part of the old Palace of Whitehall that survives. In 1829 Sir John Soane carefully refaced it with Portland stone like the original, so that the identity of the façade designed by Inigo Jones has been retained. Inside, Rubens painted nine canvas panels, which he planned in 1621 but did not complete until thirteen years later. The allegorical scenes symbolize the peace and prosperity of the reign of James I.

'Too handsome for the rest of the palace': such was the verdict of one contemporary upon the Banqueting House. Later Inigo Jones did improve the palace by adding the Clock House and a wooden stairway leading to St James's Park. He also converted the Cockpit into a theatre to replace the temporary masque-house which Charles had built behind the Banqueting House when it became apparent that the smoke of many candles and torches used in the masques would damage the painted ceiling. Yet the Banqueting House still revealed the deficiencies of the rambling and partially ruined Tudor palace. The Surveyor of His Majesty's Works, John Webb, a pupil and son-in-law of Inigo Jones, received an order from Charles I to draw up plans for rebuilding Whitehall. If the scheme which this former pupil of Wren's envisaged in his various drawings had ever been realized, London might have had a Palladian palace of a magnificence to have rivalled Versailles.

On 23 December 1641 Charles I returned an evasive answer to the Grand Remonstrance, Parliament's manifesto for reform. Stirred up by news of massacres of Protestants in Ireland and rumours of a similar popish rising about to burst out at home, multitudes of poor people from the City of London marched to protest at Westminster. On their way down the public thoroughfare from Charing Cross the mobs paused to shout their slogans outside Whitehall Palace where the King was in residence. Some roared out 'that they would have no more porter's lodge but would speak to the King when they pleased'. In these circumstances Charles thought fit to accept an offer from several hundred disbanded officers to serve as his bodyguard at Whitehall. These men, many of them veterans of the wars, loudly professed their contempt for the 'roundheads', as they called the crop-haired apprentices in the passing mob. Such insults led to fights outside Whitehall, and the apprentices came back in larger numbers to jeer at the 'cavaliers' before drifting off to Westminster.

In January 1642 Charles I left his capital to raise his standard in the north; he was not to return to Whitehall until, seven years later, he came there to die. During that time, Whitehall was left empty and desolate. 'A palace without a presence! A Whitehall clad in sable vestments!' exclaimed a Parliamentarian enthusiastically, writing towards the end of 1642. As it stood 'in a dumb silence' under its new masters, he compared it to the ruined buildings of defeated Troy. Now you could walk into Whitehall from the street and wander round, but it was a dismal experience. In the dining hall great black leather jugs sat under the tables, full of cobwebs.

Gone also were the crowds of sightseers at the gates, waiting 'to ravish themselves with the sight of ladies' handsome legs and insteps as they took coach'. In their place came soldiers in buff coats and burnished steel, marching back to their billets in the palace or manning the battery of cannon sited outside the Holbein Gate to cover the approach to Westminster from Charing Cross. To accommodate the soldiers a guard-house was erected in the tiltyard, the forerunner of the later barracks for the Horse Guards.

Shortly after one o'clock on Tuesday 30 January 1649, a cold grey winter's day, Charles I stepped out of the staircase window of the Banqueting House onto the high scaffold. One spectator wrote that he walked 'with the same unconcernedness and motion that he usually had when he entered it upon a masque-night'. Perhaps all those masques upon the semidivine nature of kings, in which Charles had played his part, were mere rehearsals for this supreme performance:

> *That thence the royal actor born*
> *The tragick scaffold might adorn:*
> *While round the armed bands*
> *Did clap their bloody hands.*
> *He nothing common did or mean*
> *Upon that memorable scene*

Yes, it would be a glorious death, Charles had assured his two youngest children some days earlier. 'I am a martyr of the people,' he said to those about him.

Charles must have felt he was standing next to paradise on that scaffold in the midst of Whitehall Palace. 'You haste to a crown of glory,' murmured Bishop Juxon to him. 'I go from a corruptible to an incorruptible Crown, where no disturbance can be,' replied the King. A vast crowd thronged the street and lined the roofs and windows of neighbouring buildings, but the high railings of the scaffold were draped with black and few saw more than the headsman's axe-blade as it swung up and down. A second executioner held up the head for all to see: 'Behold the head of a traitor!' The crowd shuddered.

Oliver Cromwell and his family moved into the main part of Whitehall Palace after he became Lord Protector, having lived earlier in some rooms at the Cockpit. His wife Elizabeth found herself the unwilling mistress of this motley collection of buildings, having expected to be the lady of no more than a modest manor house in East Anglia. According to a hostile critic, probably a sacked cook at Whitehall, she had some secret passages and trapdoors constructed so that she could spy upon the servants, whom she suspected of idleness. Not being accustomed to that 'roomy and august dwelling, and perhaps afraid of the vastness and silence thereof', Mrs Cromwell partitioned many of the rooms to make them more homely. But the family never felt at home. Cromwell's mother jumped every time she heard a musket shot, believing her son had been assassinated.

As head of state Cromwell kept his court at Whitehall. Fifty gentlemen, in uniforms of black and grey with silver lace, a troop of red-coated life guards and a retinue of servants lived in Whitehall with him. He restored most of the royal furnishings, and the palace came to muted life. Cromwell entertained ambassadors there. After a good dinner the ladies joined them for instrumental music and songs from a choir, with a psalm to round off the evening.

Despite Elizabeth Cromwell's attempts to cut Whitehall down to size, a former royal palace made an inappropriate setting for the private paradise of Puritan family life. Cromwell could have made himself king but refused to do so. When he died in 1658 he left unresolved the constitution of the nation, thus paving the way for the restoration of the Stuarts.

At Whitehall Charles II created a very different kind of paradise, dominated by the gods of pleasure. Although he lacked the funds necessary to build there Webb's still unrealized rival of Versailles, yet he lavished money upon the palace. Sorbière, a French visitor in 1665 who thought the place 'ill-built', except for the very stately Banqueting House, tells us why Charles favoured it. He called Whitehall 'a more commodious residence than the Louvre, for it contains above two thousand rooms and that between a fine park and a noble river, so that 'tis admirably well suited for the conveniency of walking and going about business into the City'.

From 1670 some new apartments at the end of the Matted Gallery overlooking the orchard were granted to a favoured mistress, Louise de Keroualle, who was created Duchess of Portsmouth in 1673. She had the rooms rebuilt and redecorated three times 'to satisfy her prodigal and expensive pleasures', noted John Evelyn disapprovingly. Her suite surpassed ten times the 'richness and glory' of Queen Catherine's apartments: Japan cabinets, pendule clocks and massive silver vases stood beneath walls hung with 'some of her Majesty's best paintings'.

Charles also gave rooms in the palace to some of his other mistresses. When Lady Barbara Castlemaine was 'in great favour' she occupied the lower floor of the Holbein Gate and some adjoining rooms. She entertained the King to supper three nights running in her suite. Even when the Thames overflowed its banks and flooded the palace kitchens, the redoubtable Castlemaine would not be deterred: the cook told Lady Barbara that her chine of beef could not be roasted that night and she flashed back a royal answer: 'Zounds! she must set the house on fire but it should be roasted!' So the joint was carried to a neighbouring house and cooked there.

Other mistresses shared the King's nightly attentions. One of them, Frances Stewart, whose lovely legs were widely admired, served her country as well as her monarch by sitting as the model for Britannia on the new coinage. But it is Nell Gwyn's name that has captured the public imagination and become a legend. William Chiffinch, the King's trusted servant, guided her and other ladies to the royal bed through a labyrinth of corridors, including doubtless some that Elizabeth Cromwell had made for more mundane purposes. With his bunch of keys and lanthorn, Chiffinch navigated a course from door to door, leading his charge for the night wrapped in her cloak. He was kept busy, for Charles lived up to his reputation. The Earl of Rochester summed up his royal master in a memorable couplet:

> *Restless he rolls about from whore to whore,*
> *A merry monarch, scandalous and poor.*

Charles seemed to have more affection for his dogs than some of the women in his life. In 1682 further building works transformed the King's private apartments near the river. A new bedchamber was provided for the King, with an anteroom hung with three tapestries depicting the adventures of Don Quixote. For these rooms he ordered 'cushions for the dogs' and a 'screen of wire, with the frame of walnut tree suitable to chairs, for his Majesty's new bedchamber, to preserve the bed from being spoiled by the dogs'.

During his brief and disastrous reign of three years James II commissioned Wren to design a new building facing the Privy Garden and extending from the Holbein Gate to the river. It included a Catholic chapel adorned with dark oak carvings by Grinling Gibbons. Nothing now remains of this building, nor of the small court and Council Chamber behind the Banqueting House. The only relic of his time is the large wrought-iron weathervane atop the latter. But James II miscalculated the prevailing political winds of his day and gusts of anti-popery swept him out of his kingdom.

The joint successors of James, his Protestant daughter Mary and her husband William of Orange, were ceremoniously offered the crown in the Banqueting House and then proclaimed at Whitehall Gate by York Herald to the assembled Lords and Commons. According to Evelyn, Mary ran about her new palace with undisguised glee, 'looking into every closet and conveniency and turning up the quilts upon the bed, as people do when they come to an inn'.

Fire, that chief enemy of palaces, always threatened Whitehall. The wide Tudor chimneys accumulated soot, and some lazy servants shifted it by firing muskets up them. From 1662 onwards a leather bucket full of water stood in every fireplace, but it took more than a few pints of water to quench the fire that broke out on 4 January 1698. Some clothing, hung up to dry in front of a charcoal fire, suddenly blazed in an upper room near the river. Fire engines pumped water from the Thames, while soldiers blew up houses with gunpowder to contain the fire and forcibly restrained those royal servants and looters intent upon rushing into the inferno to recover what valuables they could lay their hands upon.

The fire raged for seventeen hours, consuming all but the Banqueting House, the Cockpit side of the palace, the Holbein and King Street Gates and the service buildings round Scotland Yard. In the smoking ruins one looter picked up a gold bust of Cardinal Wolsey, doubtless a survival from the days of York Place. 'It is a dismal sight,' wrote a Londoner, 'to behold such a glorious, famous and much renowned palace reduced to a heap of rubbish and ashes, which the day before might justly contend with any palace in the world for riches, nobility, honour and grandeur.' William visited the site next day and declared that he would build anew, but his asthmatic aversion to the place turned his brave words into an empty promise. Wren and Hawksmoor prepared some plans but they never reached a builder's hands.

Gradually the acres of ruins were cleared and more government buildings were erected on the site of the old Palace of Whitehall. The first Admiralty had been built before the fire on the north side upon a site acquired by Queen

Elizabeth in 1560, which had served as a palace timber yard for the first twelve years thereafter. Wallingford House, which was built on the yard, came into the possession of the Duke of Buckingham three years after his appointment as Lord High Admiral in 1619, and he established a Board of Admiralty here which continued to meet after his death. No doubt because of these associations the site of Wallingford House was chosen for the building of the new 'Admiralty Office' in 1694, designed by Wren. In 1726 Ripley's new Admiralty was erected.

William Kent's Treasury (1734) arose on the place where the tennis courts and Cockpit Theatre had once stood. When the Treasury was rebuilt in 1962 workmen unearthed the foundations of one of the original Tudor tennis courts. Downing Street, which stood on the edge of the old palace, became the home of the First Lord of the Treasury. Since Gladstone's day the Prime Minister has lived in No. 10 by virtue of also holding that office. In the rebuilt Horse Guards the Commander-in-Chief's room, situated above the central carriageway, overlooked Horse Guards Parade. Various ministries on the east side of the street now sit heavily upon the memories of the courts in the palace that Charles I knew. In 1759 the Holbein Gate, a familiar landmark to Londoners for two centuries, was taken down to widen the street; its brother at King Street had been dismantled some years earlier.

Since 1920 the sovereign has stood, on Remembrance Sunday, near the site of the King Street Gate to pay tribute on behalf of the nation at the simple Cenotaph 'to our glorious dead'.

Further up Whitehall stands the bronze equestrian statue, a memorial to the execution of Charles I, 'the saddest sight England ever saw'. It was erected in 1672 on the site of the old

Charing Cross. Nearby stands the Banqueting House, stranded now among the grey office blocks and shorn of its royal function, but still reminding us of the past glory of Whitehall Palace.

5: ST JAMES'S

The winter receptacle of all the pomp and glory of this Kingdom

A view of the north front of St James's Palace, 1819

Within fifty years of the Norman Conquest a hospital for leprous women stood on the site of the present palace. Pilgrims returning from Palestine brought this disease home with them, and many similar hospitals had to be built in the countryside near large towns. In the marshy fields beyond Westminster 'fourteen leprous maiden sisters, living chastely and honestly in divine service' bore their affliction in the hospital dedicated to St James the Less, Bishop of Jerusalem. As Little St James's Day is also May Day, the fair which the hospital was allowed to hold to augment its funds became known as May Fair. In course of time the fields which once saw the annual May Fair came to hold some of the most fashionable and expensive houses in the land.

By 1532, thanks to the decline in leprosy, St James's Hospital contained only four elderly ladies. King Henry VIII had already been given Whitehall three years earlier and now he acquired this hospital from Eton College by exchanging it for other lands. He gave pensions to the ladies and rebuilt their former abode into a 'magnificent and goodly house' round four courts, and annexed to it a park which he enclosed with a wall of brick. In honour of Anne Boleyn, who stayed there often, Henry adorned the place with the initials 'H' and 'A': they can still be seen on the gatehouse with its four octagonal towers, on six other turrets in various parts of the building, on the fireplace in the Presence Chamber and in several other rooms.

Three of Henry's courts survive, known today as Ambassadors' Court, Friary Court and Colour Court. Like the Tudor buildings round the courts, the Chapel Royal has been much restored, although the painted ceiling is still substantially the work of Holbein. After Anne Boleyn had fallen from favour and met her death on Tower Green Henry came only rarely to St James's to hunt deer in the enclosed Park. Queen Mary Tudor had a great liking for the place; perhaps it reminded her of those smaller royal manors where she spent much of her girlhood. For state receptions and ceremonies she used Whitehall, but she looked upon St James's more as her private residence.

As a Roman Catholic and even more by accepting as husband Philip, King of hated Spain, Mary obstinately courted the unpopularity of most of her subjects. According to Francis Bacon, who heard it from 'a great dealer in secrets', one even tried to assassinate her as she walked in the Park 'by means of a burning-glass' held on the lead roof of the palace, but this primitive death ray had no effect. Sir Thomas Wyatt, posing as a defender of the Prayer Book, but fired more by dismay at the prospect of a Spanish king than by religious zeal, adopted less sophisticated methods, and in January 1554 led a rebellion which was probably the greatest challenge the Tudor monarchy had to face.

The campaign opened badly for the Queen and Wyatt was soon on his way to Southwark at the head of more than 15,000 men. Consternation spread through the capital, but the crisis gave the Queen an opportunity to display her abundant personal courage, and, remaining in London against all advice, she appealed to the loyalty of her subjects.

They rallied to her cause. Severe fighting took place before her eyes — she watched from a gallery in the gatehouse of Whitehall as the battle ebbed and flowed at St James's and Charing Cross. Some arrows even fell into the palace yard. But London held firm, and as darkness fell that winter afternoon Wyatt surrendered. He and his lieutenants were rounded up and taken to the Tower. The Queen had retained both her city and her kingdom.

Some four years later, deserted by Philip of Spain and finally disappointed in her longings for an heir, Mary died at St James's. Queen Elizabeth rarely stayed at the palace. Probably it was not grand enough for her. But a visitor has left us with a pleasing description of St James's in her reign:

> *Although it appears without any sumptuous or superfluous devices, yet is the spot very princely, and the same with art contrived within and without. It stands from other buildings about two furlongs, having a farm house opposite to its north gate. But the situation is pleasant, endued with a good air and pleasant prospects. On the east, London offers itself in view; in the south the stately buildings of Westminster, with the pleasant park and the delights thereof; on the north, the green fields.*

James I assigned the palace to his eldest son, Prince Henry. The young Prince became a favourite of the more Puritan-minded of his father's subjects. When only fourteen or fifteen years old he had boxes kept at his three houses — St James's, Richmond and Nonsuch — causing all who swore oaths in his hearing to pay fines into them, which were afterwards given to the poor. At St James's he played war games on a long table, with models of horse and foot regiments, as part of his programme for perfecting himself in the art of war.

Upon Henry's death at the age of nineteen his brother Charles took his place. After the accession of Charles to the throne his wife, Henrietta Maria, continued to use St James's, especially for the duty of bearing the royal children. When her mother, the Queen-Dowager of France, visited her daughter with a retinue in 1638 three people died in an anti-popery demonstration outside the gates of the palace. The French party had plenty of time to admire — and damage — the tasteful collections of paintings, furniture and tapestries which now adorned the interior of St James's Palace — they stayed two years! The second chapel in the palace, originally designed by Inigo Jones for the Spanish Infanta whom Charles was expected to marry, served as a Catholic place of worship for these combined French entourages. It is a fine building in the classical style, with Venetian glass in the east window.

In the Civil War the birthplace of the royal children became their prison. But St James's was no castle, despite the battlements that topped the brick walls. Lady Dalkeith, disguised in a torn and tattered dress, with an artificial hump made of old rags sewn on one shoulder, spirited away the two-year-old Princess Henrietta in a grubby boy's dress. James, Duke of York (later James II), who was then fifteen, escaped in girlish petticoats which his accomplices ordered from a

London tailor. He fooled his guards by playing hide-and-seek every evening for a fortnight, so that when he did let himself out into the Park on the night of his escape they thought he was 'at his usual sport'. He made his way to the coast and took a boat to Holland. His father was not so fortunate. It was at St James's that he bade his poignant farewells to his younger children, and it was here in January 1649 that he spent his last night on earth before striding briskly, under a military escort, across the Park white with hoar frost, to Whitehall and his 'second Marriage Day'. So he called his impending execution, 'for before night I hope to be espoused to my blessed Jesus'.

During the Commonwealth the palace became a state prison and a barracks. After the Restoration Charles II used St James's for state purposes, although he reserved several suites there for his mistresses. Louise de Keroualle, Duchess of Portsmouth, had rooms provided for her not only in St James's Palace but at Whitehall as well. The main part of the palace, however, was occupied by James, Duke of York. Samuel Pepys saw Lady Castlemaine there, 'who looked prettily in her night clothes'. Hortense Mancini, Duchess of Mazarine, arrived in some style to take up her lodgings in the stable yard. She was dressed as a man in full Restoration plumage, and followed by a train of retainers and dogs, together with her little page. After Hortense's death, her ghost appeared in the palace to her former companion Madame de Beauclair — one of James, Duke of York's mistresses — to warn her of impending death. It is probably the most authentic ghost story in any of the royal palaces, complete with spectral figures fading through walls.

Charles II enjoyed taking his spaniels for walks in the Park. On one occasion he offered a £5 reward in the *London Gazette* for the return of a 'liver colour'd and white spotted' spaniel answering to the name of Towser, who had made off during such a walk. The celebrated French gardener, Le Nôtre, who is said to have designed the groves and grottoes at Versailles, transformed the old Tudor hunting-park into spacious gardens covering some 36 acres. The newly constructed lake was stocked with waterfowl of all kinds, while several species of deer, as well as antelopes, elk, Guinea goats and Arabian sheep, roamed the Park. Birds of paradise in gilded cages eyed the courtiers as rivals in Birdcage Walk. On the northern side of the Park a new mall — hence the name of this wide avenue today — was formed and lined with trees so that the King and other enthusiasts for the croquet-like game of pall-mall could enjoy their sport away from the dust kicked up by the coaches in the older mall, Pall Mall. It is not surprising that fashionable men and women resorted to the Park. One winter's day Pepys followed the Duke of York into the Park, 'where, though the ice was broken, he would go slide upon his skates, which I did not like, but he slides very well'.

Between the two malls the King had granted Nell Gwyn some land to build a house, where she lived from 1670 to 1687. There Evelyn 'saw and heard a familiar discourse between the King and Mrs Nellie; she looking out of her garden on a terrace at the top of the wall, and the King standing on the green walk under it.'

After he became king, James II moved to Whitehall, but his second wife, Mary of Modena, returned to her old home at St James's to give birth on 10 June 1688 to James Francis Edward, known better to history as the Old Pretender. The Queen's timely pregnancy had aroused suspicions: Princess Anne believed her stepmother wore a 'false belly' and tried to feel it. A legend grew up that a changeling had been smuggled into St James's in a warming-pan. Some fifty people were present in the room, but the curtains of the great bed to which the suspicious warming-pan was brought remained firmly closed throughout the birth. Despite the audience of peers and privy councillors with the King, the room lacked what might be called neutral observers. So the warming-pan rumour spread unchecked and played its part in the Glorious Revolution later that year.

William of Orange stayed briefly at St James's Palace in 1688. Ten years later fire destroyed his official residence at Whitehall and St James's became its natural successor as the centre for court ceremonies. Queen Mary died childless of smallpox in 1694, aged only thirty-two, and William granted a suite of rooms in the palace to the heir, Princess Anne, and her husband, George of Denmark. When Anne ascended the throne in 1702 the palace became 'Our Court of St James's', the official royal palace of London, for Whitehall was a ruin, Greenwich a naval hospital and Kensington not to Anne's taste.

Queen Anne gave the orders for a number of additions, such as Hawksmoor's stable block to house her horses and carriages. Inside, she improved the state rooms. Queen Anne's Drawing Room, with yellow furniture and fittings, is exceptionally rich and handsome. The Throne Room contains some superb carvings by Grinling Gibbons. Here Samuel Johnson, aged three, was brought in 1712 to be 'touched for the King's Evil', an ancient ceremony, as old as Edward the Confessor, in which the royal hand was supposed to cure scrofula or struma by stroking the tell-tale swellings. Charles II had touched nearly 100,000 people, valuable work in the days before the National Health Service. As the monarch stroked each person's face or cheeks, a chaplain quoted the scriptural verse: 'He put his hands upon them and he healed them.' Then each patient received a small gold coin, engraved with an angel, to wear around the neck on a white ribbon. William of Orange would have no truck with this relic of the semidivine pretensions of kings, and referred supplicants to his predecessor, James, who continued to touch in exile. Queen Anne was the last reigning monarch to exercise these specialized healing powers. Samuel Johnson in later life had 'a confused but somehow a sort of solemn recollection of a lady in diamonds and a long black hood'.

The Queen resided at St James's every autumn and winter. Court life there was magnificent but extremely dull. Anne lacked small talk, and tended to stand in silence once she had briefly discussed the weather. But her eyes were more active than her tongue. Although she could be very familiar in the company of private friends, she was quick to spot any breaches of court etiquette. For example, she identified anyone not wearing a proper full-bottomed court wig and sent over an attendant to tell them to go back home and fetch one. Nobody was allowed to wear spectacles, and smoking was banned even in the Mall. Games of cards relieved the monotony in the evenings, probably much more than did the court jester, the first to be appointed for more than a century. As Lord Chesterfield wrote, 'her drawing-rooms were more respectable than agreeable, and had more the air of solemn places of worship than the gaiety of a Court'.

Queen Anne insisted upon the sort of court protocol that the Tudors, with their elevated notion of kingship, had required of their subservient households. As in the days of Queen Elizabeth, her servants addressed her on their knees. The daily rituals dated back for centuries. For example, according to the authority of Mrs Masham, the Queen's constant companion:

When the Queen washed her hands, the page of the backstairs brought and set upon a side table the basin and ewer; then the bedchamber woman set it before the Queen, and knelt on the other side of the table over against the Queen, the bedchamber lady only looking on. The bedchamber woman poured the water out of the ewer upon the Queen's hands... The page of the backstairs was called in to put on the Queen's shoes. When the Queen dined in public the page reached the glass to the bedchamber woman, and she to the lady in waiting.

Queen Anne, like Henry VIII, was plagued by woman-troubles. Against the backcloth of this formal court at St James's, the two chief protagonists for her favour — Sarah, Duchess of Marlborough and Mrs Abigail Masham — fought out their petticoat war of looks, silences and angry words. When Sarah finally stormed out to the newly completed Marlborough House, throwing down her keys as Mistress of the Robes, she 'left that part of the palace, which had been her headquarters for years, in a state as if it had been sacked by a destructive enemy — the locks torn off the doors, marble slabs forced out, and looking-glasses and pictures rent from their panels.' Sarah also applied for £18,000 in settlement for her unpaid salary, compensation enough, she said, for hours of boredom at court. To her credit, Anne gave her these arrears of pay. It seems that in a royal palace paradise has always existed more in the imagination of visitors and onlookers than among those chosen to experience the reality.

George I, Queen Anne's successor in 1714, brought his own household staff from Hanover to St James's. His favourite mistress, Ermengarde von der Schulenburg, whom he created Duchess of Kendal, occupied a splendid suite in the palace. To arrange a further supply of nocturnal companions the King relied upon the services of his two Turkish attendants, Mustapha and Mahomet, who brought something of the atmosphere of an Eastern harem to the red-brick Tudor building. Not that George lacked mistresses; and the fatter the better. 'These standards of his Majesty's taste,' wrote one contemporary, 'made all those ladies who aspired to his favour strain and swell themselves like frogs in the fable. Some succeeded, and others burst.' No queen had to witness these antics, for his divorced wife, Sophia Dorothea, was safely locked up in a German castle.

George did not subject himself to the rigours of learning English and spent half his time in Hanover. The English ways puzzled him. 'The first morning after my arrival at St James's,' he wrote, 'I looked out of the window and saw a park, with walks, and a canal, which, they told me, were mine. The next day Lord Chetwynd, the Ranger of my Park, sent me a fine brace of carp out of my canal, and I was told I must give five guineas to my Lord Chetwynd's servant for bringing me my own carp, out of my own lake, in my own Park.'

Domestic harmony still eluded the palace. George quarrelled bitterly with his eldest son, the Prince of Wales, later George II; he in his turn found it impossible to get on with his own heir, Prince Frederick. St James's was the scene of perhaps the most spectacular of their many family rows. In 1737 Frederick's wife became pregnant. Queen Caroline, who wanted the succession to go to her second son William, suspected trickery and resolved to be present at the birth. The labour pains began prematurely at Hampton Court and at once Frederick took his wife by coach to St James's, where she gave birth to a tiny girl. Back at Hampton Court servants awoke Queen Caroline at two in the morning with the news and within minutes the angry mother-in-law was on her way to St James's to inspect her grandchild. She would say nothing to her son, but kissed the baby and muttered in French, 'The good God bless you, poor little creature, you have arrived here into a disagreeable world.'

After this incident George decided to expel the Prince of Wales from St James's, declaring, 'I thank God tomorrow night the puppy will be out of my house.' The Queen added, 'I hope in God I shall never see him again.' Nor did she, for later that year the fifty-five-year-old Queen took to her deathbed in the palace. Her doctors tried several medicines to no avail, such as 'Daffy's Elixir', mint-water, whisky, snake root and even Sir Walter Raleigh's cordial, which Raleigh had concocted when he was a prisoner in the Tower and had sent across to St James's in the hope of saving Prince Henry's life. She lingered on, with her doctors letting blood copiously to ease her fever. No wonder she called one of them 'you blockhead!' After her death the King told an attendant, 'I never yet saw the woman worthy to buckle her shoe.'

The long-standing quarrel between George II and his heir did not, however, greatly mar the spectacle which the King and Queen were at pains to create at St James's so that the public could admire the smiling face of royalty and indulge once more in the fantasy that life in royal palaces transcended their more mundane existence. Visitors could even buy tickets for an enclosure where they could watch the royal family eat their Sunday dinner on gold plate, waited upon by liveried servants. At levées men only were received, while at 'drawing-rooms' ladies were presented to the sovereign. These took place on Mondays and Fridays and the King appeared regularly, looking, towards the end of his reign, 'a severe little old gentleman with white eyebrows and a red face'.

Conscious always of the glories of Versailles, many Englishmen felt rather ashamed of St James's Palace. In George I's reign Daniel Defoe thought it too mean to be 'the winter receptacle of all the pomp and glory of this Kingdom'. In his opinion even the petty princes of Europe had better palaces. In 1776 Sir John Fielding was equally scathing: 'The buildings that compose this merely nominal palace, (for by all the rules of architecture it has no claim to the title), are low, plain and ignoble, devoid of any exterior beauty to attract and fix the beholder's eye. It reflects no honour on the kingdom and is the jest of foreigners.'

In 1760 Prince George succeeded his grandfather and moved into St James's from Savile House. He was not well known to his subjects, but he quickly won approval and popularity by his good nature and evident desire to please people. 'I saw him again yesterday,' wrote Horace Walpole, 'and was surprised to find the levée-room had lost so entirely the air of the lion's den. This young man don't stand in one spot, with his eyes fixed to the ground and dropping bits of German news; he walks about and speaks to everybody.'

The following year the eighteen-year-old Princess Charlotte of Mecklenburg-Strelitz came to St James's to wed the King. She trembled when she first set eyes on the palace from her coach. Seeing the Duchess of Hamilton smiling at her anxiety, Charlotte said, 'You may laugh; you have been married twice; but it is no joke to me.' Certainly being married to George III was far from a joke, but the couple were destined to have some happy years. They were married that very day. Charlotte wore a violet mantle of ermine which was so heavy, noted Walpole, 'that the spectators knew as much about her upper half as the King himself'.

Shortly afterwards, George III purchased Buckingham House for his queen, and it eventually became their private residence in London. Yet St James's remained in use for state occasions, levées and dances, such as Queen Charlotte's Birthday Ball when debutantes were presented to the Queen. Royal christenings and weddings still took place there, including that of the Prince of Wales to Princess Caroline of Brunswick, whom he had agreed to marry to clear his debts.

Prince George had taken an intense dislike to his bride at first sight; at the wedding he did not bother to disguise his agitated distress at having to endure her company. 'He was like a man in despair, half crazy,' wrote an eyewitness. 'He held so fast by the Queen's hand she could not remove it... the Duke of Gloucester assured me the Prince was quite drunk, and that after dinner he went out and drank twelve glasses of Maraschino.' It is hardly surprising that when the Prince became George IV he did not care much for St James's. However, he did add a state room, a fine banqueting hall, and also improved the Park.

It was here that Queen Victoria married Prince Albert, before some 300 guests who crammed into the Chapel Royal to witness the historic occasion. Although she was to live at Buckingham Palace, St James's remained the headquarters of court ceremonial. The Lord Chamberlain had his offices there, together with the central chanceries of the orders of knighthood. The Marshal of the Diplomatic Corps arranged the ceremonies in the Presence Chamber when ambassadors presented their credentials to the sovereign. In 1865 Queen Victoria gave up the custom of holding drawing-rooms there, but levées continued to be held until the end of George V's reign.

Today, except for the battlements, St James's looks like an Oxford college that has become somehow stranded in the fashionable West End. Its grander neighbour, Buckingham Palace, seems to overshadow it. Yet St James's has never ceded precedence to the Regency upstart. The Queen receives foreign ambassadors at Buckingham Palace, but they are still accredited officially to her Court of St James's. Junior members of the royal family, such as the Duke of Kent, continue to reside in the palace, and heralds still proclaim the accession of a new monarch in Friary Court. Though no longer 'the winter receptacle of all the pomp and glory of this kingdom', St James's remains a storehouse of royal memories.

6: GREENWICH

Neptune's hall

The Queen's House and the Greenwich Hospital in the painting London from Greenwich Park, in 1809, by William Turner

On 21 January 1698, a distinguished visitor arrived incognito in England. He was Peter the Great, Tsar of Russia. William III received him with much civility and gave him lodgings in the capital. One evening, when dining with King William at St James's Palace shortly after a visit to Greenwich — then a naval hospital — he was asked what he thought of Sir Christopher Wren's building. 'Extremely well, sir,' he replied. 'If I were permitted to advise your Majesty, I should recommend you to remove your court thither, and convert your palace into a hospital!'

The Tsar may not have known that in the Middle Ages, in the days when St James's was still a leper hospital, a royal palace stood at Greenwich. Henry V obtained the manor in the loop of the Thames when he confiscated the endowments of the alien priories in 1414: the manor of Greenwich had been in the hands of the Abbey of St Peter of Ghent for more than five centuries. Humphrey, Duke of Gloucester, King Henry's youngest brother, became Regent during the minority of Henry's son and heir, and received a grant of the manor, building himself a large house there, which he called 'Bella Court'. With battlements, towers and a moat it could withstand siege, a prerequisite in the troubled 15th century. A small outlying castle, known later as Duke Humphrey's Tower, commanded the strategic road from Dover to London.

After Humphrey's arrest for high treason and his subsequent death in prison, Bella Court passed into the hands of Queen Margaret of Anjou, the spirited wife of Henry VI. She changed its name to the Palace of Placentia or Pleasaunce. She brought a feminine touch to the stone building, paving the floors with terracotta tiles which bore her monogram and glazing the windows with expensive glass. Sculptors adorned the pillars and arcades with her emblem, the ox-eyed daisy known as the marguerite. A vestry was built to house her jewels. West of the house she had constructed a pier in the river so that the royal barges, each pulled by twenty oarsmen, could arrive or leave whatever the state of the tide. Breezes from the river kept the palace fresh. On the land side an enclosed Park of heath held plenty of game for royal hunting parties.

After 1485 Henry VII changed the name of the buildings yet again to Greenwich Palace and gave them a new face of red brick. It was here that Henry VIII was born and by the end of his reign the palace had taken an imposing shape. The rooms stood around three quadrangles by the river: the Fountain, Cellar and Tennis Courts. The main gateway stood opposite Queen Margaret's Pier. Henry added a tiltyard and armoury, besides some fine rooms in the palace itself. Holbein received four shillings a day to paint the ceiling of the new Banqueting Hall. The King's gardeners made the lawns, ponds and orchards into the finest in the land. It was a fitting palace for what Henry intended to be the most glorious reign that England had ever seen.

In 1516 King Henry was twenty-four, still in the springtime of both his life and his reign. He stood more than 6 feet tall, a splendid figure of a man. Proud of the shapely calf of his sturdy legs, he once took the Venetian ambassador aside to assure him that the new French king, although as tall as himself, did not have as fine a calf. His flaxen hair had darkened and thinned early, so it was 'combed short and straight in the French fashion'; the paucity of it was hidden in his portraits by a flat bejewelled black cap trimmed with white fur.

The young King loved hunting, and would ride at Greenwich from dawn until dusk, tiring out eight or ten horses in a day's chase. He went hawking there as well, sometimes hurling himself across obstacles with a fenman's vaulting pole as he followed the birds. He played tennis, 'at which game it is the prettiest thing in the world to see him play, his fair skin glowing through a shirt of the finest texture.' In the Park he practised the martial sports: wrestling, throwing the 12-foot spear, fighting with blunt two-handed swords, shooting the longbow, and casting the light and heavy bars. Above all, he enjoyed performing in his new tiltyard, before an admiring audience, jousting with such spirit and skill that he overcame all opponents and outshone all rivals.

The early years of Henry's reign saw the court at play in rounds of colourful pageants, feasts, revels, jousts and tourneys. Six months after his marriage at Greenwich to Catherine of Aragon, for example, Henry rushed into the Queen's suite dressed as Robin Hood, with ten companions in short jerkins of 'Kentish kendal', and danced with the ladies, who pretended to be much taken aback. Some days later he made a sudden reappearance at a banquet given for foreign ambassadors as a mysterious Eastern emissary dressed 'in Turkey fashion', hung with gold ornaments and wearing two scimitars at his side. Six courtiers dressed as Prussians accompanied him, while black-faced 'Moors' held the blazing torches. Minutes afterwards Henry, now dressed like a peacock in a brilliant suit of blue and crimson, re-emerged in order to dance with the ladies. Three years later he took a leading part in the first masque, an Italian invention not seen before in England, in which the performers wore velvet masks over their faces.

From the windows and lead roofs of Greenwich Henry loved to watch the large vessels of London bringing in silk and gold, or carrying out wool and metal. Here, too, he could visit his ships of war anchored close to the palace. Many of these warships were built at the two new naval dockyards, Woolwich and Deptford, which flanked his palace.

With her memories of the clear skies and warm airs of Spain, Catherine of Aragon never liked living in Greenwich Palace. Soon after her arrival in England, the cold grey mists of the Thames invaded the red-brick courts and induced in her shivering fevers and racking stomach aches. Later Greenwich became the melancholy setting of her repeated failures to bear

King Henry an heir. Eventually she had a daughter, Mary, who was baptized at Greenwich. Yet no sons appeared. In time Henry's desire for a son, coupled with his passion for Anne Boleyn, led to the divorce from Catherine of Aragon and the break with the Church of Rome.

On 29 May 1533 Anne Boleyn savoured her triumph: a coronation procession by water from Greenwich. It was perhaps the most magnificent pageant of that colourful reign. A flotilla of more than 300 barges and smaller boats waited to accompany the new Queen to the Tower. The Mayor and Aldermen of London in their scarlet robes sat in their resplendent barge.

The Bachelors' sailing barge, ablaze with cloth of gold, bore two great banners with the arms of the King and Queen at bow and stern, while the flags of the Haberdashers' and Vintners' livery companies bedecked the sides. Rows of tiny bells in the rigging added their sounds to the string music and trumpet flourishes which arose incessantly from the fleet. A light galley carried a huge painted cloth dragon, moving backwards and forwards spouting fire. At last the gay procession set out up river and brought Anne to the Tower. She rode in Catherine of Aragon's barge, Catherine's arms having been effaced. Henry met her at the Tower and escorted her with pomp to Westminster Abbey where she was crowned.

Alas for her, on 7 September Queen Anne gave birth at Greenwich Palace to a daughter, Elizabeth. Henry was bitterly disappointed. As the months passed, suspicions gathered about his wife's reputation and the gossip eventually penetrated Henry's jealous mind. On May Day in 1536 the brooding King exploded into action. That day Anne took her place beside Henry in the gallery of the tiltyard to watch the jousting below. Her brother, Lord Rochford, and Sir Henry Norris, the King's groom, rode out in their gleaming armour. The knights thundered towards each other, divided only by the fence that ran the length of the yard: the lances splintered and snapped on impact. Perhaps Anne's looks or cries of encouragement betrayed her. Suddenly the King arose and departed with six attendants by barge to London. What did it mean? The next day, after a fitful night of worry, Anne found herself being interrogated by the Privy Council under the Duke of Norfolk. There she was, as she said, 'cruelly handled at Greenwich by my Lord of Norfolk'. The charges were incest with her brother and adultery with four other men. Norfolk, her uncle, kept shaking his head at her answers and saying, 'Tut, tut, tut'. Meanwhile, Norris, one of her suspected lovers, had become a prisoner in the Tower. Anne soon joined him there and endured the ordeal of having to watch while they were all executed. Her own execution followed, on the third anniversary of her coronation: she had been Queen of England for 1,000 days.

In due course Anne's daughter succeeded to the throne as Elizabeth I. She frequently kept her court at Greenwich, a palace her mother and father had both loved. In the first year of her reign a contingent of the London militia, 1,400 strong, held a muster in the Park to entertain her.

Some years later this spot was the scene of a famous incident. The young Walter Raleigh, bearing despatches with news that the Spanish invasion of Ireland had failed, saw the Queen for the first time in his life, standing before a 'plashy place' at the rear gatehouse of the palace. Determined to make an impression, he flourished out his cloak to cover the puddle and knelt as the Queen stepped upon it. Later the young Captain of the Guard, as he became, joined the ranks of those who flirted with the Virgin Queen. Using a diamond, he is said to have etched a window at Greenwich with the words: 'Fain would I climb, but that I fear to fall.' Beneath them, Elizabeth added: 'If thy heart fail thee, climb not at all.'

Like her father before her, Queen Elizabeth loved to stand at the windows of Greenwich and watch tall ships heeling to the wind in the Thames or slipping down river on the ebb tide. Her half-sister Mary had narrowly escaped with her life when one vessel, observing the royal standard floating from the walls, fired the customary salute. By an oversight the gun was loaded and the ball crashed through her apartments 'to the great terror of herself and her ladies'.

In June 1576 Martin Frobisher, with three small ships, sailed down river bound for North America. 'Outside the palace at Greenwich,' wrote Richard Hakluyt, 'they dressed ship and shot off their ordnance, while the Queen waved her hand to them from a window.' Frobisher brought back a Red Indian couple. A German visitor to Hampton Court in 1592 saw 'life-like portraits of the wild man and woman' hanging among the Queen's collection of masterly paintings, the first Americans so honoured.

Four years later the Queen witnessed the safe return of the *Golden Hind* after the first circumnavigation of the world. Drake sailed his ship past Greenwich and saluted the Queen before anchoring at Deptford. Elizabeth dined on board ship with Drake and knighted him on his own quarterdeck. The *Golden Hind* was moored permanently at Greenwich and (much like the *Cutty Sark* today) became a fashionable attraction for Londoners. The astrolabe which Elizabeth presented to Drake that day can still be seen at Greenwich.

Foreign visitors were much impressed by Greenwich. The Austrian ambassador wrote to inform Archduke Charles, a suitor for Elizabeth's hand, that it was an incomparable palace.

As she had some twenty other such royal summer residences, he added 'she is well worth the trouble'.

At Christmas in 1585 Leopold von Wedel watched her dine in public, amid much processing, bowing and kneeling from the attendants and courtiers. When she washed her hands, three earls edged towards her on their knees holding the large silver basin. After dinner Elizabeth sat on a cushion to watch the dancing, chatting and jesting most amiably with the young men. 'Pointing with her finger at the face of Master or Captain Rall [Raleigh], told him there was a smut on it. She also offered to wipe it off with her handkerchief, but he anticipating her removed it himself.' As Sir Walter Raleigh, this same man would land at Greenwich in 1618 after his voyage to Guinea. Ten weeks later Elizabeth's successor ordered his head to be struck off for offending Spain. 'Fain would I climb…'.

In 1618 King James I gave the palace to his queen, Anne of Denmark, as a present to mark their reconciliation after a quarrel. She commissioned Inigo Jones to build her a small palace on the site of the back gatehouse. Thus the Queen's House stood astride the Deptford to Woolwich road, linking the gardens to the north with the Park on the south side. The road actually ran beneath a 30-foot archway joining together the two buildings which comprised the house, so that the Queen would be able to walk into either gardens or Park at will. The finished Palladian building, one of the finest examples of that style, centred upon a magnificent black and white marble paved entrance hall. This hall was in the shape of a giant 40-foot cube, a theme which the architect developed later with his vast double-cube Banqueting House at Whitehall. The new role for the hall as a reception room, which Inigo Jones pioneered here, deeply influenced English domestic architecture, the only subsequent innovation thereafter being the bringing of the main staircase into the hall itself.

As Anne of Denmark died in that same year she never lived in her country palace. A decade or so later Charles I gave the manor to Henrietta Maria, who ordered Inigo Jones to resume work on it. On the south side six Ionic pillars graced an elegant loggia, forming what Inigo Jones called 'a frontispiece in the midst' and giving an expansive view across the Park. The delicate balustrade above gave the flat roof a regal crown. Jones also designed the interior fittings, such as the fireplaces and the lavishly carved wooden friezes. Upon the first open-well spiral staircase in England, Jones placed a graceful wrought-iron balustrade with fleurs-de-lys in honour of the Queen. Gentileschi adorned the ceiling of the ground entrance with his nine canvas panels depicting the Arts of Peace, while paintings by Rubens, Titian, Raphael and Van Dyck hung upon the walls.

The marble tablet — 'Henrica Maria Regina 1635' — above the middle window-head on the north side records the completion of the house. Because of its lime-rendered walls it was known as the 'White House'; the Queen's own affectionate name for it was the 'House of Delight'. Possibly that name was inspired in part by a splendid tapestry in the Queen's Drawing Room by the Flemish artist Jacob Jordaens: it depicted the loves of Cupid and Psyche. Certainly the royal couple spent many happy weeks at Greenwich. On 18 May 1635, for example, the Venetian ambassador could inform his masters: 'On Wednesday last his Majesty went to Greenwich with the Queen. It is thought that they will both stay there at least six weeks, the King to enjoy the pleasures of the chase and the Queen to see the completion of a special building of hers which is already far advanced.'

During the Commonwealth the old palace buildings served partly to provide rooms for Cromwell's ministers and partly to house Dutch prisoners-of-war. Bulstrode Whitelocke, the Parliamentarian lawyer and politician, who became a close associate of Cromwell, seems to have lived in the Queen's House for a while, possibly at the suggestion of the Lord Protector, for whom the house was reserved.

After the Restoration the workmen of Charles II knocked down the neglected medieval buildings of the old palace by the river. John Webb supervised the enlarging of the Queen's House, which became once more the home of Henrietta Maria, now the Queen Mother. She lived there in some style, with twenty-four gentlemen in black velvet coats and embroidered gold badges, each carrying a halberd, to escort her when she went by sedan chair to chapel or to meals.

On the site of old Placentia, the King laid the foundations of a new palace, to be called the King's House, but shortage of money hampered progress. Samuel Pepys, who often visited the shipyards nearby, wrote in his diary: 'I go to Greenwich by water and landed at the King's House, which goes on slow but is very pretty.' During the reign of Charles II only the west wing was completed. In the Plague of 1665 it served as a refuge for the Board of Admiralty.

Following plans drawn up by Le Nôtre, who never came to England, the gardens were re-styled in the formal French manner. A 'snow well' was built there: probably the first deep-freeze in England. On Castle Hill, using the foundations of Duke Humphrey's Tower, Wren built the red-brick Royal Observatory. The King established it in 1675 for the purpose of determining more accurately the position of the stars. This knowledge was to be especially useful for improving navigation, an essential art for a seafaring nation. Sir John

Flamsteed, the first Astronomer Royal, had to buy most of his instruments out of his annual salary of £100. Not until twelve years later could he afford an assistant. Flamsteed spent much time quarrelling with Isaac Newton, who was impatient to get his hands on the tens of thousands of stellar observations made at Greenwich.

When William and Mary came to the throne in 1688 there had been no work done on the King's House for ten years. With their own building programme in mind, which included Kensington Palace and some major changes at Hampton Court, the joint sovereigns had no interest in completing it. Queen Mary adopted an earlier proposal for making the King's House at Greenwich the basis for an infirmary for old and wounded seamen of the Royal Navy, a counterpart in fact to the Royal Hospital for disabled soldiers at Chelsea. It had to be a grand building, worthy of the nation's heroes, and one that Louis XIV's magnificent Les Invalides could not outshine.

In 1692 the important Battle of La Hogue, a five-day encounter at sea when the Royal Navy destroyed the French fleet, brought the plight of disabled British seamen into the limelight. To commemorate the victory, Queen Mary distributed £30,000 among the fleet and announced her decision to found Greenwich Hospital.

In true patriotic spirit Wren would accept no fee for drawing up plans for the new hospital. From the first it was more than a hospital: that was only the excuse. It was a statement of national pride. 'The buildings at Greenwich are far too magnificent for a place of charity,' said Dr Samuel Johnson with his usual bluntness. For, after Mary's death in 1694, William looked upon Greenwich as a memorial to her and it was built like a palace. Wren's original scheme, for receding and ever-narrowing courtyards, with a domed building to close the vista, was rejected in favour of an arrangement that framed the elegant Queen's House. Mary had insisted that a strip of land, some 115 feet wide, was kept clear from her beloved Queen's House to the banks of the river, and her wishes were respected. Yet the Queen's House was really too small to provide a centrepiece for Wren's Baroque buildings. Dr Johnson told Boswell he thought the resulting compromise 'too much detached to make one great whole'. When Canaletto painted Greenwich in about 1750, with artistic licence he subtly faded it out into the distance.

The Greenwich Hospital buildings stand as a commanding monument to the genius of Sir Christopher Wren. The artist Sir James Thornhill painted the ceiling of Wren's Great Hall. As it took nineteen years to finish, it included a scene of the historic arrival at Greenwich in 1714 of the first Hanoverian king, as well as the central theme of William and Mary handing the Cap of Liberty to Europe. In fact George landed late one night by torchlight, having been rowed up the Thames from the royal yacht in a pea-soup fog, but Thornhill painted him being borne from the river in a chariot, dressed in a toga like a triumphant Roman emperor.

Thornhill also painted himself in the foreground, beckoning the viewer with outstretched hand — some said he was holding it out for more money. Although he received £3 per foot for the ceiling, he petitioned for more in the hope 'that this being an Hospital will make no difference, since Royal Hospitals are as well embellished as Palaces, and with as much expense'.

As for the Queen's House, it sank lower in royal esteem. Queen Anne allowed Sarah, Duchess of Marlborough, to remove Gentileschi's ceiling paintings to Marlborough House. The house became the official residence of the Rangers of

Greenwich Park and a reception house for distinguished visitors. In 1699 the Earl of Romney, who was Ranger at the time, coolly diverted the public Deptford to Woolwich road from under his house, a deed that no law-respecting monarch had attempted.

In 1806 Caroline, Princess of Wales, finally sold her Ranger's rights at Greenwich to a naval charity for use as a school for seamen's children. Four years later, colonnades were built on either side, where once the cobbled road had run, linking two new wings which housed the pupils. The Queen's House continued as a school until 1933 when the National Maritime Museum was established there.

The old school gymnasium contains among other treasures a gilded 17th-century state barge. Perhaps the most memorable object in the museum, however, is the uniform coat which Nelson wore when he was shot at Trafalgar.

Before the end of the 19th century the Royal Naval College replaced the naval hospital in Wren's building. Today Greenwich is both a working museum and college, but it retains the air of a palace.

7: BRIGHTON

Oh, this wicked Pavilion

The richly decorated Banqueting Room at the Royal Pavilion,
from John Nash's *Views of the Royal Pavilion*, 1826

In September 1783, the future George IV — then just twenty-
one and Prince of Wales — travelled to the south coast in his
coach to stay with his uncle, the Duke of Cumberland, in the
small fishing town called Brighthelmstone. Cumberland had
'discovered' Brighton, as it became known, four years earlier,
when his physician had recommended it to him as a health spa.
Apart from the bracing sea breezes, there was plenty of salt
water to be drunk hot as a tonic, mixed with milk and a dash of
tartar sauce. Medical writers argued that Brighton seawater
contained more salt, the town standing away from a river
mouth. The heir to the throne had been told that draughts of

such salubrious seawater might clear up the glandular swellings on his neck, which he sought to disguise behind especially high collars and stocks.

'His Royal Highness's arrival,' reported the *Sussex Weekly Advertiser*, 'was announced by the ringing of bells and a royal salute at the battery, where, unhappily, through some indiscretion in reloading one of the pieces, it went off and wounded the under-gunner mortally. His body was blown off the battery to some distance on to a bank.' The Prince presented a few guineas to the dead man's family, and appeared that evening at a glittering ball in richly embroidered silk coat. There were horse and coach races, with wagers upon the results. Tommy Onslow won twenty-five guineas from the Prince for driving his light carriage twenty-five times at a gallop through two narrow gateways without touching. With such companions he gambled, danced, wenched, ate and drank to his heart's content.

Far from his father's eye, the Prince had enjoyed his playground at Brighton so much that the following year he leased a house near to Cumberland's and close to the Steine, a broad grassy stretch of land on the eastern edge of the town where fishermen spread their nets to dry and fashionable visitors promenaded in order to take the air and to be seen. According to one biographer, it was more than the taste of salt water laced with milk that drew George back to Brighton that summer. He was enticed 'by the angelic figure of a sea-nymph whom he one day encountered reclining on one of the groynes on the beach'. The young lady responded to his advances, but like many such holiday affairs, their relationship was destined to be a brief one.

The Prince soon built himself a spacious red-brick house in the classical Palladian style on the site he now rented from its new owner, his Clerk of the Kitchen. Designed by Henry Holland, the 'Marine Pavilion' was centred upon a domed saloon, with bow-windowed wings to north and south. This building is still the nucleus of the Pavilion today and is represented by the present Saloon, and the North and South Drawing Rooms. The south wing was divided originally into a breakfast room and anteroom, balanced in the north wing by a dining room and library. The Prince's bedroom, on the first floor of the south wing, was decorated with quilted chintz and green and white chequered silk bed hangings. The room was fitted with a large mirror so placed that George could lie on his bed and watch the promenade on the Steine.

In 1785 George had secretly married a young and comely Roman Catholic widow, Mrs Maria Fitzherbert, 'the wife of my heart and soul'. During his frantic courtship the Prince had even rolled on Charles James Fox's floor (according to Lord Holland), sobbing and crying that if he could not live with her in England 'he would abandon the country, forgo the crown, sell his jewels and scrape together a competence to fly with her to America'. Instead he took her to Brighton. Though the Pope recognized their marriage, it was not regarded as legal in England. Heavily in debt, the Prince temporarily abandoned the rebuilding of Carlton House in London and sold his string of racehorses as marks of his married austerity.

Soon the Prince's favourite Whig politicians came to see him in the Marine Pavilion. They mixed with his other friends, such as that paragon of elegance Beau Brummell. As an arbiter of society's taste, Brummell insisted upon perfectly cut clothes in quiet colours, complemented by the finest snowy linen. Only in the evenings would he condone the Prince and his friends dressing like birds of paradise. Doubtless thanks to Beau Brummell, the Prince became the best-dressed man in Europe

— with the exception of Brummell himself — but in doing so he spent another small fortune.

> *'Tis at Brighton, the mirror of watering places,*
> *Assemble their Honors, their Lordships and Graces,*
> *Nay, England's first Prince — and the famous Dame*
> *Fitz.*
> *And old friends meet new friends of fashion and wits.*

Parading themselves in new clothes, racing, gambling and practical joking — these were the main occupations of the Prince and his cronies. Cricket games took place on the Steine, the Prince batting and bowling 'with great affability and condescension'. A character called 'Smoaker' Miles acted as his 'dipper' or swimming teacher. It is said that one rough day Miles stood in front of the Prince to prevent him venturing into the treacherous currents. 'What do you think your father would say to me if you were drowned?' he demanded. 'The King would say,' replied George, enjoying the imagined scene, 'this is all owing to you, Smoaker. If you'd taken proper care of him, Smoaker, poor George would still be alive.' There may have been times when George III would have not cared overmuch if Smoaker had neglected his duty one windy day…

While the 'Terror' raged in Paris during the French Revolution, after the fall of the Bastille in 1789, the Prince and Mrs Fitzherbert would often wait on the beach to welcome aristocratic *émigrés* who had fled the guillotine and entrusted their lives to small fishing smacks. Many of these French aristocrats found temporary refuge in the Pavilion before moving elsewhere to join friends or relatives. Meanwhile, red-coated regiments trained on the South Downs near the town to safeguard England from the fatal storm across the Channel.

'Oh, this wicked Pavilion,' wrote the Whig politician, Thomas Creevey. 'We were there till half-past one this morning and it has kept me in bed with the headache till 12 today.' Part of the trouble was the immense patent stove which heated the house like an oven, so that when fires were lit in the evening the place became unbearably hot. The Prince, an advanced hypochondriac, believed that the place should be steaming hot for the sake of his health, just as he also had himself bled copiously. Sheridan once lent across the table and asked one of the Prince's cronies, George Hanger, how he felt. 'Hot, hot, hot as hell,' replied Hanger. 'It is quite right,' said Sheridan, 'that we should be prepared in this world for that which we know will be our lot in another.'

Not all guests were prepared, however, for the Prince's disconcerting methods of keeping his guests awake. George liked firearms and airguns. After dinner he was inclined to shoot up the place, like some drunken frontiersman in his father's dominion of America. His aim was unpredictable, especially when he had drunk several bottles of claret: he and a friend once sent the orchestra diving for cover as they shot at the glass chandeliers. Generously he proffered the guns round the table; some guests made excuses but on one such night, 'Lady Downshire hit a fiddler in the drawing-room, Miss Johnstone a door, and Bloomfield the ceiling.'

The Prince had not applied himself with any enthusiasm to the task of cutting down his expenses. By 1795 he owed nearly £640,000, a huge sum in those days. In return for having his debts paid off, the Prince reluctantly agreed to marry Caroline of Brunswick, an ordeal he performed at St James's with the help of 'Dutch courage' from the bottle. The pair were hopelessly incompatible and soon separated, even before the birth of their daughter, Princess Charlotte. In 1800 Mrs

Fitzherbert returned to him, having obtained permission from the Vatican to do so. That year the Prince bought the estate upon which the Marine Pavilion stood.

'Prinny' then embarked upon a programme of alterations to the house, sign of things to come. Green-painted tent-shaped metal canopies appeared over the wrought-iron balconies along the classical front, like mushrooms overnight. A Chinese gallery was formed to house the gift of some Chinese wallpapers, together with a painted glass passage-room which gave the visitor the impression he was walking through a giant-size Chinese lantern. The Chinese look spread rapidly throughout the house, consuming the cartloads of chinoiserie which arrived from London: lacquered cabinets, bamboo furniture, models of junks, porcelain vases, rolls of wallpaper, silk screens and incense-burners.

Although he had just added new rooms and changed the decorations, the Prince was already dreaming of an Eastern palace. At first he contemplated 'a stately pleasure dome' in the Chinese style, but he veered away from that idea. Possibly he realized, as Humphrey Repton said later, that the Chinese manner, although decorative for interiors, was too light and trivial for architecture, except of course for small garden houses such as the Pagoda at Kew. The Chinese plans laid aside, the Prince's workmen began building the magnificent royal stables, now the Dome, together with the coach houses and Riding School on the north side of the estate. A house was built for Mrs Fitzherbert on the Steine, which survives to this day despite much rebuilding. By 1808, when the work on the stables neared completion, observers could see the first fruits of a new influence at work, a spirit which would soon transform the whole exterior of the Pavilion — the Islam-inspired architecture of India.

In 1805 the Prince had inspected some designs he commissioned from Humphrey Repton for building the main house in the new style. He declared them to be perfect and decreed to the architect that 'not a tittle shall be altered'. Nine years passed, however, before the Prince's dire financial straits would allow him to return to his grand scheme. In 1811 he had become Prince Regent and six years later he appointed Repton's partner, John Nash, as his Surveyor-General. Nash, the architect of the great Regency programme of building in London, produced some new drawings for the Pavilion. Probably as a result of conversations with the Prince Regent, a man of good artistic judgment and creative flair, Nash gradually moved away from any strict adherence to Indian patterns. He produced designs for a selection of Oriental domes and minarets, pinnacles and cupolas, which delighted his royal client and caused dismay to the more prosaic taxpayers.

Perhaps the best commentary upon the ideas behind the Pavilion comes from the Romantic poets of the day. Coleridge, for example, drew upon the same sources for his vision of Kubla Khan's 'stately pleasure dome' in Xanadu, where 'the milk of Paradise' was to be drunk. A year later Thomas Moore published his best-selling poem *Lalla Rookh*, which evoked the splendour of the Mogul court set in the paradisical valley of Kashmir, where

> *… the magic of daylight awakes*
> *New wonders each minute as slowly it breaks.*
> *Hills, cupolas, fountains, call'd forth every one*
> *Out of darkness as if but just born of the sun.*

Thus the Pavilion was a reaction against the tradition which located the golden age in Greece or Rome, symbolized by

Renaissance and Neoclassical architecture. China and India offered new riches in their different ancient traditions of how and where kings should live. They stood for the rosy dawn of emotion and colour after the long pale night of reason and order. For those imaginations jaded with classical ruins the domes and minarets of the East seemed more than picturesque — they were sublime.

Among the first of Nash's buildings to be completed was the Great Kitchen, a showplace replete with the latest gadgets of the Industrial Revolution. Four iron columns, disguised as palm trees with leaves of bronze, supported its lantern roof. A vane rotating in the chimney turned the roasting spits before the open fireplace. Other contrivances stood ready for boiling, baking, stewing, frying, steaming and heating food. The Prince liked his food hot, so there were hot plates, hot closets, hot air, hot hearths and large tanks of hot water on tap. In December 1816 the stone pavement was covered with scarlet cloth and the Prince Regent and a select party of his friends sat down to eat supper with the servants for a joyous hour, which delighted them all, 'particularly the female portion'.

The new light-green Entrance Hall and Long Gallery or Corridor, profusely decorated in the Chinese style, were completed in time for the visit of Princess Charlotte, now twenty, in January 1816. On this occasion, the Prince Regent accepted his estranged daughter's choice of a husband. Next month he met the young man, Prince Leopold of Saxe-Coburg, at the Pavilion. He received him in the Entrance Hall, surrounded by walls painted in pink and green, with dragons on the panels. Chinese lanterns threw a soft light on the rich profusion of chinoiserie which greeted the German Prince as he made the acquaintance of his future father-in-law.

The principal and most magnificent of the state apartments — the Banqueting and Music Rooms — were both begun under Nash's direction during the following year and completed in 1820, the year when the Prince Regent became King George IV. The ceiling of the Banqueting Room, domed under an external tent-like roof, is painted to seem like an Eastern sky. Below it hangs a silvered dragon holding in its claws a glittering chandelier 30 feet long and weighing almost a ton. It was one of the first chandeliers to be lit by gaslight rather than candles. The whole room cost more than half a million pounds to furnish.

The Music Room rivalled the Banqueting Room in Oriental splendour, with its great domed ceiling set with countless carved and gilded scales, cunningly arranged to give an illusion of greater height. On formal evenings after dinner an orchestra played, its members dressed in Turkish clothes. Distinguished singers, such as the tenor Kelby, sang here for the guests; the King summoned Kelby's little daughter from her perch behind the orchestra and sat her on his knee. On another occasion he received the Italian composer Rossini in the Music Room. Often, after most of the guests had gone home, George would entertain his more intimate friends with songs in his fine baritone voice, interspersed with the gossipy stories he told so well. On such nights, he told Lady Granville, he cried for joy when he reflected on the delights of the Pavilion.

Late at night the King would retire to his new private apartments, consisting of anteroom, library and bedroom. The head and foot of his bed were stuffed and covered with silk; white satin pillows, swansdown blankets and a fine white Marseilles quilt lay on top of it. White marble lined the bathroom, which contained a bath 16 feet long, 10 feet wide and 6 feet deep. Pumps and other machinery supplied it with salt water from the sea.

Mrs Fitzherbert had long since been compelled to share George's affections with a succession of elderly and handsome mother-figures, such as Lady Hertford. Gradually Mrs Fitzherbert found her position untenable. In 1811, when she was invited to a grand fête at Carlton House to celebrate the occasion when George became Prince Regent, she found no seat reserved for her at the high table. Rather than meekly joining the throng at the buffet tables, she confronted her husband and asked him where she was to sit. 'You know, madam, you have no place,' said George. 'None, Sir, but such as you choose to give me,' replied Mrs Fitzherbert with some dignity.

Lady Bessborough, another matronly grandmother, succeeded Lady Hertford and elicited a display of passion from the Prince which owed much to the romantic mood of the day. In a letter she described his ardent wooing. She saw his antics through the realistic eye of a mature lady who was long since past the age when she cared to be assaulted by a royal version of Lord Byron:

He threw himself on his knees and, clasping me round, kissed my neck before I was aware of what he was doing. I screamed with vexation and fright; he continued, sometimes struggling with me, sometimes sobbing and crying... vows of eternal love, entreaties and promises of what he would do — he would break with Mrs Fitzherbert and Lady Hertford, I should make my own terms, I should be his sole confidante, sole adviser... I should guide his politics, Mr Canning [whom Lady Bessborough favoured] should be Prime Minister...; then over and over again the same round of complaint, despair, entreaties and promises... that immense, grotesque figure flouncing about, half on the couch, half on the ground.

The exotic appearance of the Pavilion inevitably gave rise to rumours of an Oriental pursuit of pleasure inside its walls. In his earlier days there, the Prince Regent doubtless cultivated this Byronesque atmosphere of magnificent luxury. Indeed, he admired the poetry of Byron, who incidentally came to stay in Brighton during this time but has left us no record of his impressions of the Pavilion.

Writing in a letter from the Pavilion, Princess de Lieven, the wife of the Russian ambassador and a close friend of 'Prinny', found the theatrical atmosphere distasteful: 'There is something effeminate in it which is disgusting. One spends the evening half-lying on cushions; the lights are dazzling; there are perfumes, music, liqueurs — "Devil take me, I think I must have got into bad company." You can guess who said that, and the tone in which it was said.'

Charles Greville, who was Clerk to the Privy Council from 1821 to 1860, visited the Pavilion and wrote his impressions in his *Journal*. He records how an evening in the Pavilion fell far short of that vision of carefree, private, informal pleasure that had no doubt inspired the Prince Regent to build it. Reclining on his cushions or swapping stories late at night with his cronies in the Music Room, George may have tasted the reality for an hour or so. But after he had become king, as Greville suggests, the Pavilion swiftly succumbed to that ever-lurking enemy of those who sought to experience paradise on earth in the splendid surroundings of the royal palaces — boredom.

'The gaudy splendour of the place amused me for a little and then bored me,' wrote Greville. 'The dinner was cold and the evening dull beyond all dullness. They say the King is anxious that form and ceremony should be banished, and if so it only proves how impossible it is that form and ceremony should not always inhabit a palace. The rooms are not furnished for society, and, in fact, society cannot flourish without ease; and who can feel at ease who is under the eternal constraint which etiquette and respect impose?'

Greville's question is a good one, applicable to all the royal palaces. For he had put his finger on a central dilemma for any monarch wishing to create a noble court. Hence Greville's feeling of strain and ennui, despite the fact that 'the King was in good looks and good spirits, and after dinner cut his jokes with all the coarse merriment which is his characteristic.'

As the King gradually lost interest in Lady Hertford his affections mounted in particular for another lady from much the same mould. The Marchioness of Conyngham, who was fifty-one in 1820, moved into the Pavilion with her husband and five children. While the Marquess and two sons busied themselves in the minor offices found for them, Lady Conyngham kept the King happy. Whether she did this service as companion or mistress is much disputed and matters not at all. Certainly what George needed was security and affection: she treated him as the loveless, lonely and spoilt schoolboy that he always remained. In return he would do anything for her, even abandon the Pavilion, which she probably found too redolent of Mrs Fitzherbert. Indeed, the Duke of Wellington later recalled that the King deserted his Pavilion by the sea because Lady Conyngham, having read 'some words on a window written with a diamond and reflecting severely upon herself, declared in her passion that she would never return to the palace — nor did she, nor the King either'.

Possibly George abandoned Brighton in 1827 because he felt that he had exhausted all the creative possibilities of the Pavilion. Wyatville's equally romantic transformation of Windsor into a Gothic fairy-tale castle or Nash's rebuilding of Buckingham Palace may have caught his imagination. More probably, he longed for greater privacy than a developing Brighton town could offer, a place where he could take the air in his open carriage away from those prying eyes inspecting his gross, gout-ridden body.

Towards the end of his life he spent much of his time at the Royal Lodge in the Great Park at Windsor, a modest house which Nash had created from a cottage before he began work on the Pavilion. When George became seriously ill with dropsy in Windsor Castle it was the Lodge, not the Pavilion, that he missed. 'Ah, the poor cottage, I shall never see it again,' he said in June 1830, not long before he died.

William IV, who succeeded him, brought Queen Adelaide to Brighton for a part of every summer during his reign. As third son of George III, William had not expected to sit on the throne. When he was Duke of Clarence he had pursued an eventful naval career, rising to be an admiral. It seems that the bluff old sailor — he was sixty-five in 1830 — looked upon the Pavilion, where he had spent many happy days as a younger man, as a man o' war moored in port, with a large crew that had to be kept busy. Life there, writes Greville, was 'very active, vulgar and hospitable; King, Queen, Princes, Princesses, bastards and attendants constantly trotting about in every direction'. Mrs Fitzherbert was made an honorary member of the crew, as Mary Frampton relates in her diary of 1831:

> The magnificence of the parties given by the King and Queen at the Pavilion at Brighton is spoken of as realising the ideas of the entertainments described in the 'Arabian Nights', the dinners consisting daily of about forty persons. The King is very temperate. He consults Mrs Fitzherbert much as an old friend in matters relating to the fêtes, etc.

William offered her the title of Duchess, which she refused, perhaps because Brighton always treated her as a queen. Significantly, she did accept the privilege of clothing her servants in the royal livery. She obviously enjoyed being visited in her house on the Steine by the King and then receiving her first invitation back to the Pavilion. 'I felt rather nervous,' she told her adopted daughter, 'never having been in the Pavilion since I was drove away by Lady Hertford. I cannot tell you of my astonishment at the magnificence and the total change in that house since my first acquaintance with it.' But the sparkling eyes, pouting lips and upturned nose of the Prince Regent, with his preposterous enthusiasm and endless talk, had given way to stolid Hanoverian domesticity. Despite much formal entertaining, 'they lead a very quiet life — his family the only inhabitants. I think I counted eight Fitz Clarences.'

William IV intended to have the Royal Pavilion recognized as an official royal palace. Invitations to services in the royal chapel during his reign were headed: 'Palace, Brighton'. But the romantic mood which had inspired this version of Coleridge's 'sunny dome of pleasure' was already fading. Change and progress became the watchwords, and that meant Europe rather than the static if colourful civilizations of the Orient. Tennyson, a young man of twenty-one when George IV died, would capture the new marching spirit in his words:

> *Not in vain the distance beacons. Forward, forward let us range.*
> *Let the great world spin forever down the ringing grooves of change.*
> *Thro' the shadow of the globe we swept into the younger day.*
> *Better fifty years of Europe than a cycle of Cathay.*

In Brighton the Chain Pier, built about three years before George IV left the town forever, symbolized the age of progress which was dawning. The Pavilion was the first house to use cast-iron pillars in its construction, but they supported an essentially backward-looking dream. The sweeping iron arches and chains of the pier rested upon the same principles of engineering as the suspension bridges, such as those at Clifton, Bristol, and the Menai Straits. George IV is said to have gone for a last farewell drive along the seafront and ordered his carriage to halt while he surveyed the pier once more with distaste. Then, turning away with a shudder, he gave word to be driven to Windsor. William IV, who lacked his imagination, enjoyed tramping up and down the Chain Pier almost every day, for he thought it resembled the deck of a ship — 'the most delightful place in the world'.

When Queen Victoria visited Brighton Pavilion four months after her accession she thought it 'a strange, odd Chinese looking thing, both inside and out'. From one of her sitting room windows she could just see 'a little morsel of the sea'. Although the Queen came again to Brighton in 1838 and each summer from 1842 to 1845, usually accompanied by the Prince Consort and their young children, she felt no affection for the place. Above all, the crowds which always gathered whenever the Queen stirred out of the Pavilion irritated her as the years went by. 'The people are very indiscreet and troublesome here really, which makes this place quite a prison,' she concluded.

For Prince Albert and Queen Victoria, like George IV in old age, any paradise on earth included the essential ingredient of privacy, where the quiet pleasures of family life could be enjoyed away from the glare of public duties. The Royal Pavilion, stuck in the middle of the growing seaside resort of Brighton, could not provide that privacy. So in 1845 Victoria and Albert purchased Osborne House on the Isle of Wight, which thereafter served as their private seaside home. In 1850 the Pavilion was sold to the town of Brighton for £50,000, less than a tenth of its original cost, and in the fulness of time the Corporation opened its restored halls to the public. Today the Royal Pavilion stands as a memorial to the extraordinary King who created it.

8: HOLYROOD

Scotland's bloodstained palace

A view of the palace and abbey in 1789

'Justice, justice! Save my life, madame, save my life!' The ghostly shouts of David Rizzio reach us across the centuries as his murderers drag him out of the presence of Mary, Queen of Scots. The events of that appalling night of 9 March 1566 seem to have impressed themselves into the very walls of Holyrood Palace, giving it a sombre air. We have to imagine it in earlier and happier years, with the sun shining upon the granite château and bringing to life the hills round it.

The Palace of Holyrood or Holyroodhouse took its name from the abbey built in 1128 by King David I, a mile from the protecting arm of Edinburgh Castle. The abbey owed its name to a fragment of the True Cross or 'Rood', a relic which acted like a magnet to pilgrims from all over Scotland. Canongate, the way from the abbey to the castle, was so called because the monks of Holyrood were Augustinian canons.

In the Middle Ages, when they visited Edinburgh, Scottish kings usually stayed within the thick stone walls of the castle, secure as the eagles high upon the craggy hills behind. Coronations and marriages, births and funerals, often took place in Holyrood Abbey. Gradually the monarchs formed the custom of lodging in the abbey's guest house, which stood on the west of the main buildings towards Edinburgh. The court ladies, in particular, must have found these quarters more to their taste than the cramped castle bailey. Moreover, the position of the abbey at the base of Arthur's Seat and Salisbury Craigs was sheltered from the east winds, making possible leisurely walks and sports in the gardens.

James IV, one of the most popular of Scottish kings, chose Edinburgh as the capital of Scotland and decreed that the Holyrood Abbey guest house should become a royal palace. It was there that he married Margaret, daughter of Henry VII of England, in 1502. At that time Scotland had close ties with France — the basis of the military alliance against the English that Henry VII was attempting to undermine by uniting 'the Thistle and the Rose' in marriage. The French influence shows in the architecture of Holyrood: James IV's great north-west tower, which still stands, has the pointed turrets rising above a crenellated parapet characteristic of the royal châteaux of France.

During the minority of his young son, James V, workmen added a south wing to the great tower, with a main door set between two semi-circular towers. But the plan called for another great tower and wing on the other side of a quadrangle to balance this range and the buildings were not finished. During the fighting with England, the palace suffered considerable damage. The English general, the Earl of Hertford (later Duke of Somerset and Lord Protector), marched into Scotland with orders to 'sack, burn and slay'. This punitive campaign was to include the taking and sacking of the town of Edinburgh, together with the royal castle and palace. Hertford's soldiers looted the palace and set it on fire, but the massive stone walls of James IV's tower shrugged off the flames. Nor did it prove too difficult to repair the remaining buildings once the English had marched home.

Holyroodhouse will be forever linked with the name of Mary, Queen of Scots. James V and his second wife Mary, daughter of the Duke of Guise, were the parents of this noble and fascinating woman. A few days after the disastrous defeat of his army at Solway Moss by an English army, her unfortunate father died at Falkland Palace in Fife. Just before his death James heard the news that he had fathered a daughter. 'It cam' wi' a lass, and will gang wi' a lass,' he muttered prophetically. For the Stuarts had succeeded to the throne through marriage and Mary was destined to be the last Queen of Scots.

Mary was born in the palace of Linlithgow, which stood by a loch in West Lothian, halfway between Holyrood and Stirling Castle. James V had enlarged Linlithgow round its quadrangle, furnished the rooms richly and given it to his queen as a dower house. She loved the palace, perhaps because it reminded her of those distant châteaux by the Loire. It was an appropriate birthplace for a girl who became both queen of France and queen of Scotland.

In 1558 the young Mary married the heir to the throne of France. When her husband, soon to be Francis II, died two years later, she resolved to return to Scotland and landed there in August 1561. She was now a young woman of nineteen and most attractive to her contemporaries: tall (5 feet 11 inches), with thick auburn hair, a fine pale complexion and hazel eyes. Above all, she possessed that indefinable magic of charm. This charm, together with a gentle voice and naturally good manners, made her a most feminine and winning person.

The Scotland that welcomed her was a rough and violent country, especially to those in her train accustomed to the civilized ways of Paris. The Abbé de Brantôme, for example, found the Queen's reception at Holyroodhouse by the burghers of Edinburgh far from pleasing: 'there came under her windows five or six hundred citizens, who gave her a concert of the vilest fiddles and little rebecs, which are as bad as they can be in that country, and accompanied them with singing psalms, but so wretchedly out of tune and concord that nothing could be worse.'

Brantôme wrote enthusiastically about Mary: she was 'a true goddess' in beauty and grace. Even the Scots, when they heard her speak at the opening of Parliament, exclaimed, 'Vox Dianae!' ('The voice of a goddess'). Such a goddess needed a palace, a paradise upon earth. Few of the Scottish royal residences in her day could be described as palatial. But several generations of royal builders, inspired by French models of Renaissance architecture, had given Holyroodhouse a certain elegance. Mary chose it instinctively as her principal residence in Scotland. Here, like her cousin in England, she intended to present herself as a benevolent and glorious ruler, appointed by God to command her people's love, as well as their loyalty.

There were two obstacles that she faced that were unique to Scotland. First, by tradition the Scots nobility held a low doctrine of kingship: their sovereign was simply 'the first among equals'. Secondly, the psalm-singing citizens of Edinburgh who had greeted her were disciples of Edinburgh's minister, John Knox, the formidable Protestant Reformer who felt himself called to be the nation's equivalent to John Calvin in Geneva. Mary was a devout Roman Catholic. On her first Sunday in Holyroodhouse she ordered mass to be said in the royal chapel. A large crowd from the town soon gathered outside the chapel doors and turned nasty. One seized the altar candles from a terrified servant; another snatched some popish ornaments. These the crowd noisily kicked about, while inside the Queen and her French attendants heard mass, the priest shaking so much with fear that he could hardly complete the service.

The Queen summoned John Knox to meet her in Holyroodhouse, ostensibly to account for a sermon he had preached against the mass but really to size up the man. Knox arrived at the Presence Chamber, dressed in his black Genevan gown and with a long flowing beard, looking like some Isaiah or Jeremiah from the pages of the Old Testament. He was forty-seven years old, a man of dauntless courage, his mind tempered in countless theological debates, his body seasoned by a spell ten years before as an oar-slave in the galleys of France. He had returned to Scotland less than two years in advance of Mary, but in that time he had ensured the triumph of the Reformation in his native land.

At their first meeting, Lord James Stewart was the only other person present. Knox's attitude to sovereignty sounded both new and dangerous to Mary; in the midst of their speech 'the Queen stood still as one amazed more than quarter of an hour, and her countenance was changed'. Lord James asked her, 'What hath offended you, madam?' At length she said to Knox, 'Well then, I perceive my subjects must obey you and not me, and shall do what they please and not what I command.' Knox replied, 'It is my care that both princes and subjects obey God.'

The meeting ended when she was called to dinner; each parted musing on the character of the other. 'If there be not in her,' Knox said afterwards to his friends, 'a proud mind, a crafty wit and an indured heart against God and his truth, my judgment faileth me.'

Secure in the protection of the Protestant lords, Knox had no qualms in debating as an equal with his Catholic sovereign, whom he regarded — as all Puritans would — as an agent of the devil. Her charm, reason and tears, deployed in their four further conversations, could not move him and their dialogue proved fruitless. Next year Mary had her granite adversary tried for treason, but he was acquitted.

On lesser mortals the Queen's charming talk, composed of such ingredients as subtle flatteries, hints of possible attendances at sermons and avowals of conscience, worked like magic. When Lord Ochiltree arrived in Edinburgh he was greeted by Robert Campbell:

> Now, my lord, you are come, and almost the last of all. I perceive the fiery edge is not of you. But I fear you will become as the rest when the holy water of the court shall be sprinkled upon you. For I have been here now five days. At first I heard every man when he came say, 'Let us hang the priest!' But after they have been twice or thrice in the Abbey all their fervency was cooled. I think there be some enchantment at the court whereby men are bewitched.

After Mary's second marriage in 1565 to Henry Stuart — Lord Darnley — Knox preached a sermon which predictably gave great offence to the royal couple. Darnley, four years younger than Mary, was a tall and handsome youth with Tudor blood in his veins, but he was not able to command her respect. His dissolute behaviour soon cured her of any lingering infatuation for him. Darnley, being too stupid or too conceited to divine the real cause, blamed the Queen's French attendants for alienating her from him — in particular David Rizzio, the musician who also served as her secretary. The arrogant, ugly little Savoyard was widely suspected of being Mary's lover and detested by the Scots. In league with the Protestant 'Lords of the Congregation' Darnley made plans to perpetrate the worst crime ever performed in a palace in the British Isles in the presence of the sovereign — the brutal murder of Rizzio.

Mary's state apartments can still be seen today much as they were upon the night of Rizzio's murder. Her four rooms lay in the great north-west tower on the second floor. At the head of the main staircase stood a spacious Presence Chamber hung with black velvet, with the arms of the Queen's mother Mary emblazoned upon the ceiling. It led into the Queen's large bedchamber, which in turn had two small rooms at each corner, about 12 feet square, one for dressing and the other, draped in crimson and green, for dining. On the floor below, Darnley had a similar suite of rooms. A narrow private staircase linked the floors, the door opening into the Queen's bedchamber close to the dining room. (This staircase is now concealed behind panelling, the present one being a later addition.)

That Saturday evening Mary ate her supper in the company of Rizzio and others in the small dining room by the light of candles and a blazing log fire. Suddenly Darnley appeared, closely followed by Lord Ruthven, 'lean and ill-coloured', for he had risen from his sickbed to lead the attack. His armour and naked sword caused instant alarm. 'Let it please your Majesty,' said Ruthven, 'that yonder man David come forth of your privy chamber where he hath been overlong.' As all their voices rose in heated argument, Rizzio tried to fade into the background behind the curtains in the window, but Ruthven's five accomplices — armed to the teeth with swords, pistols and daggers — rushed in, pushed over the table and dragged the little Italian away from behind the Queen's skirts. As they manhandled him through the bedroom and Presence Chamber to the head of the main stairs he could be heard screaming, *'Justizia, justizia! Sauvez ma vie, madame, sauvez ma vie!'* Fifty or sixty dagger thrusts eventually silenced him and the corpse was thrown down the winding stairs.

Aware now of the deadly conspiracy against her, Mary remained cool. Next morning she craftily worked upon Darnley, who was now in a state of guilt-ridden shock. The following day, after some clever play-acting of clemency for the benefit of the conspirators, Mary made her escape from Holyrood. At midnight Darnley accompanied her down the same privy stairs where Ruthven and his men had appeared fifty-two hours previously. They found their way along the back passages to an exit near the cemetery of Holyrood Abbey, horses awaiting them. The Queen, in an advanced state of pregnancy, rode pillion behind an equerry for five hours through the night. Eventually they reached the safety of Dunbar Castle.

'No more tears now; I will think of revenge,' Mary had murmured to herself when one of her ladies told her that Rizzio was dead. After the birth of her baby, James, she had revealed her true feelings to Darnley: 'I have forgiven, but never will forget!' Remembering the loaded pistol brandished recklessly at her that night by Andrew Ker of Fawdonside, one of Ruthven's gang, she asked him, 'What if Fawdonside's pistol had shot, what would become of him and me both?'

Not long afterwards, Darnley fell sick in his own Lennox Stuart country at Glasgow, probably of syphilis. The Queen gave orders for him to be removed to Edinburgh and he chose for himself a house in Kirk o' Field, on the outskirts of the town and about three quarters of a mile from Holyrood. The Queen joined him for music and card-playing on the evening of Sunday 9 February, together with her chief nobles. One of them, the Earl of Bothwell, then reminded her that she had promised to attend a wedding-masque back at the palace. At about two o'clock in the morning she was awoken in Holyrood by a terrific explosion, a crack like the sound of twenty-five cannon fire together. Darnley's house had been blown up. Someone had strangled Darnley in his nightshirt, probably as he was trying to escape from the mined house. As Mary had said the night before, 'It was about this time of year that David Rizzio was killed…'.

After Bothwell's acquittal for the murder of Darnley, he carried off Mary to Dunbar Castle and married her. A powerful faction of discontented nobility rose against them and a year later Mary found herself compelled to take refuge in England. Here, as next in line of succession, she became the focus of Catholic plots against Queen Elizabeth. She was tried, sentenced to death and beheaded on 8 February 1587.

James VI of Scotland, Mary's son, spent much of his reign quarrelling with the nobles and the ministers of the kirk. His pedantic learning earned him the name Solomon; his more scurrilous subjects held that it derived from being a 'son of David'. In 1589 he married Anne of Denmark, granting her the palaces of Linlithgow and Falkland in the marriage settlement. He spent much money in preparing Holyrood for her reception and she was crowned queen amid much pomp in the abbey there.

In 1603 James succeeded to the English throne, taking south with him his high doctrine that kings were appointed by God and not chosen by their people. Such an idea called for splendid palaces to express it. Consequently, James ordered Holyrood to be refurbished before his last visit there in 1617. He was not disappointed, for an English visitor who saw it that year could report: 'I was at his Majesty's Palace, a stately and princely seat, wherein I saw a sumptuous chapel most richly adorned with all the appurtenances belonging to so sacred a place or so royal an owner.' These included pleasant gardens and a Park where the King could indulge his passion for hunting. Thomas Fentoun, keeper of the Park, had charge of the King's lion, tiger, lynx and game-cocks, which were presumably kept in the 'wild bestial'.

Charles I visited Holyrood in the eighth year of his reign, when he came to be crowned king of Scotland. Six Scottish bishops officiated at the ceremony, which was held in the royal chapel at Holyrood. The King paid his second and last visit during the Bishops' War, which was the result of his attempt to impose the Book of Common Prayer upon the Scots.

In 1650 Cromwell used the palace as a barracks for his soldiers, and a fire that year destroyed the greater part of it. It was Charles II who determined to rebuild the medieval pile. Working from plans drawn up by John Mylne, his workmen demolished the west front. In 1671 Sir William Bruce laid the foundation stone for the new building. Robert Mylne, John's nephew, received orders to incorporate Doric and Ionic pillars in the building. His gracious classical façade was flanked by the surviving tower of James IV — scene of Rizzio's murder — and a new south-west one which was built to balance it.

Charles II did not himself stay at Holyrood when he came to Scotland, but his brother James, Duke of York, stayed there when the bitter struggle over the Exclusion Bill — whereby he was excluded from the succession — made his absence from

London wise if not expedient. This neglect of their northern kingdom by the later Stuarts disappointed the proud Scottish people. An Englishman who visited Scotland reported that the Scots anticipated that when their palace at Edinburgh was complete the King would 'leave his rotten house at Whitehall and live splendidly amongst his own countrymen'.

In the Forty-five Rebellion Charles Edward Stuart captured Edinburgh without losing a man and took possession of Holyrood Palace. On 17 September, the day of his entry, James Hepburn of Keith stood at the palace gate and saluted the Young Pretender as he arrived at the head of a cavalcade of eighty jaded soldiers in Highland dress. 'Bonnie Prince Charlie' was a slender young man, some 5 feet 10 inches in height, with large brown eyes and red hair concealed at that time under a powdered white wig. He smiled frequently as the vast crowd made the courtyard ring with their cheers. James Hepburn, who had been out with the Old Pretender in 1715, observed that Charles Edward commanded great respect from his soldiers as 'a gentleman and a man of fashion, but not like a hero or a conqueror'. Yet two days later Prince Charles marched out to win a victory at Prestonpans.

For six weeks after Prestonpans the Prince held court at Holyroodhouse while the Highlanders camped at Duddingston. Like a sovereign he dined in public and touched for the King's Evil. At a grand ball held in his honour, his Jacobite supporters danced with their ladies, who wore the white cockade, badge of rebellion, on their dresses. As drams of whisky were poured down thirsty throats the pipers played such tunes as, 'When the King enjoys his own again'. That song, written in 1643, was as much a lament for palaces as for kings:

Though for a time we see Whitehall
With cobwebs hanging on the wall
Instead of gold and silver brave,
Which formerly 'twas wont to have
With rich perfume
In every room,
Delightful to that princely train,
Which again you shall see
When the time it shall be
That the King enjoys his own again.

Holyroodhouse, Scotland's Whitehall, saw for those weeks the nervous gaiety and butterfly splendour of the last Stuart court to be held in these islands. That brief enjoyment of 'his own' came to an end when the young Prince marched away from Holyrood, cheered by an 'infinite crowd', on his disastrous invasion of England.

The following January the 'Butcher' of Culloden, the Hanoverian Duke of Cumberland, stayed at Holyrood on his march northwards to the battle and its aftermath, where he carried out the deeds which earned him his odious nickname. Suddenly the Forty-five was over. Charles fled through the heather to Skye, finding shelter in caves and bothies. After five months as a fugitive he bade his few followers farewell and left Scotland's shores forever. Among the 'comebacks' he schemed over, he even considered raising the standard of rebellion again in America, but nothing came of it.

In 1822, George IV made a tour of Scotland and held a levée at Holyrood. Not to be outshone by Charles Edward Stuart as 'a man of fashion', the former Prince Regent arrayed himself in the kilt and plaid of Stuart tartan, like a Highland chieftain. Sir Walter Scott advised on the dress and ceremonies for the day.

When George IV's niece, Queen Victoria, visited Holyrood twenty years later, the state apartments were still not fit for royal occupation. Even her levée, planned for the afternoon in the Throne Room, had to be held at Dalkeith on account of a scarlet fever scare. Still, she inspected the palace, including the room where 'poor Queen Mary was supping when poor Rizzio was murdered'. She judged it to be 'a princely and most beautiful place'. Perhaps because it reminded her 'forcibly and sadly of former days', she spent less than a week there throughout the rest of her reign.

Queen Mary, wife of George V, restored the interior with great attention to detail. Once a year the Lord High Commissioner resides there for the General Assembly of the Church of Scotland. In this century kings and queens have stayed occasionally at Holyroodhouse, which still retains the full status of a royal palace.

9: KENSINGTON

This poor old palace

A view of Kensington Palace from 1751.

'Do you wish to see me dead?', asked King William III, when one subject remonstrated with him for moving from Whitehall to Hampton Court. After the bloodless Glorious Revolution it became clear that William's life was more in danger from the London smog than from Jacobite reactionaries. Smoke from thousands of fires burning Newcastle coals, the stench of open sewers and damp fog on the Thames conspired against the King's asthmatic chest. He spent his nights at Whitehall or St James's coughing and fighting for breath. His doctors doubted if he would last a year.

In the summer William and Mary found the atmosphere less polluted at Hampton Court, but river mists could still invade the quadrangles during the winter months. Thus the royal pair wanted a seat for the winter, closer to Whitehall than Hampton and well away from the river. William made an excursion to Kensington and looked over Holland House and Nottingham House. Eventually he chose Nottingham House, which stood empty at the time. The second Earl of Nottingham, leader of the Tory Party, obligingly sold his house, gardens and park to the King and Queen for 18,000 guineas. Sir Christopher Wren prepared drawings for enlarging the house, a commission which he discharged promptly so work could begin without delay.

Nottingham House was a small, oblong residence built in the reign of James I. Wren enlarged it by adding four wings or 'pavilions', one at each corner. He altered the face of the building by placing the main entrance on the west under a two-storeyed portico, approached through a courtyard guarded by a gate-tower. There were no grand flourishes, and the King was always to refer to it simply as Kensington House.

Work began in July 1689 and proceeded at such a pace that six months later the King and Queen were in residence. They were in such a hurry that both architect and workmen took serious risks to please them. On 7 November some of the buildings collapsed under the weight of their new lead roofs and killed a few of the workmen. Mary, who stayed at Holland House during the rebuilding, had been in those buildings shortly before on one of her visits to hasten the workmen. She interpreted the accident as a divine reproof for her bursting impatience to be at the place, 'and I was truly humbled'.

While William led his army in Ireland against her father James, defeating him eventually at the Battle of the Boyne, Mary kept him informed of progress. 'I have been this day to Kensington,' she could at last report, 'which looks really very well, at least to a poor body like me, who have been so long condemned to this place [Whitehall] and see nothing but water and wall.'

At Kensington she looked forward to seeing sweeping gardens out of her windows. With the King she created there 26 acres of flower beds in the formal French style, set with box and yew. Beyond the gardens lay the Park. In the spring of 1690 Evelyn saw the house which the King had altered. It was still a 'patched building', he thought, 'but with the garden, however, it is a very sweet villa, having to it the Park and a straight new way through this Park'.

A section of this coach-way is still visible today in 'Rotten Row' (Route du Roi). It was a wide avenue, set with posts at intervals, from which lanterns could be hung. For in those days Kensington still lay in the countryside and a minister visiting the King in his sedan chair or coach might well find himself waylaid by footpads. The lamps were lit at dusk when the court was in residence at Kensington, a welcome sight on foggy autumnal evenings.

In 1691 a fire destroyed the new south wing while William and Mary were in residence. Fortunately, it did not damage the King's Gallery, undoubtedly the finest of the new rooms. In it hung a marvellous collection of pictures. Evelyn, who saw the palace again in April 1696, called it 'very noble tho' not great'. He mentions specifically visiting 'the Galleries furnished with all the best pictures of all the houses'.

William and Mary had no children of their own, but they enjoyed children's company. The Duke of Gloucester, Anne's son, was a particular favourite with the King. At the age of four, playing at soldiers, he paraded a contingent of small boys in military uniform for his uncle's critical inspection at Kensington. The King treated the occasion with proper gravity and probably overdid his compliments, for the young Duke solemnly told him: 'My dear King, you shall have both my companies with you to Flanders.' Two years later, the King saw Gloucester drilling with a short musket and received a royal salute. 'I am learning my drill that I may help you to beat the French,' the boy said, much to William's amusement. Soon afterwards he bestowed upon his nephew the Order of the Garter, but sadly the boy died in 1700, a few days after his eleventh birthday.

William kept a traditional and stately court. 'No godhead, but the first of men,' he refused to touch for the King's Evil or wash feet on Maundy Thursday, but he employed the 'Cock and Cryer', or 'Cock of the Court', a nightwatchman who wandered round calling the hours.

In 1694 Mary succumbed to smallpox at Kensington. She was thirty-two. When she fell ill everyone who had not had the illness was ordered out of the house. The King and Queen had identical suites of rooms with separate entrances, emphasizing the fact that they were joint sovereigns, but now William moved into Mary's room and slept at nights on his camp bed. The doctors eventually gave him such a certain prognosis of death that he could not check his tears. Towards the end, William found the harrowing experience too much for him and collapsed with mental exhaustion. When he himself died at Kensington eight years later, from pneumonia contracted after a fall from his horse at Hampton Court, a gold ring containing some strands of Mary's hair was found tied to his left arm on a black ribbon.

Despite the fact that she had detested her brother-in-law William — she privately called him 'Mr Caliban' — Queen Anne chose to make Kensington her principal palace in London rather than St James's. Like William, Anne's husband, Prince George of Denmark, suffered from asthma. Kensington offered her clean country air, together with seclusion in the gardens. As the palace contained twin sets of apartments of equal status, the King's and Queen's, she could live in Mary's suite without being unduly reminded of Dutch William. After the great fire destroyed much of Whitehall, she proposed extending the palace at Kensington to provide more regal accommodation, but nothing came of this idea.

Queen Anne, an ardent gardener, made most of her changes in the acres of gardens round the palace. 'I know my heart to be entirely English,' she assured her first Parliament. It was her best card, in gardening as in politics. She set about replacing the symmetrical patterns of hedges, flowerbeds and uniform rows of shrubs with something more characteristically English. All the box hedges and bushes were uprooted first, possibly because the Queen disliked the smell from them so much. In the enlarged 'upper garden' to the north of the palace, Henry Wise and his assistants — described by Joseph Addison in the *Spectator* in 1712 as 'our heroick poets of gardening' — transformed the unsightly hollow of an old gravel pit into a wooded arbour of uncommon beauty. The gardens began to look less contrived, with vistas of grass, flowers and English trees relieving the battalions of Dutch tulips from their annual sentry duty.

In order to enjoy the gardens more, Anne resolved to build for herself a stately red-brick 'greenhouse' with round domes at each end. Wren, Vanbrugh and Hawksmoor all seem to have played a part in designing it. The resulting Orangery, with its Renaissance-inspired Corinthian columns, both exhibits the Queen Anne style of architecture and perhaps expresses the spirit of Anne's England as no other building does.

On many afternoons Anne would take tea in the Orangery, which served also as the Summer Supper House. Here the

Queen and her guests could eat dinner in air heavy with the scent of lemon and gum trees, exotic plants and flowers. On such evenings a small orchestra played discreetly in the background, hidden by the shrubs.

It was at Kensington Palace that the friendship between Anne and Sarah, Duchess of Marlborough — 'Mrs Morley' and 'Mrs Freeman' as they called each other in their letters — began to turn sour. Politics played a part, for Sarah was always pushing the Whigs and their policies towards her Tory-minded sovereign. Sarah Jennings was about four years older than Anne, who was six when they first met. In 1678 she became the wife of John Churchill, later Duke of Marlborough. A bossy, dominant woman with a violent temper, she could not take it when she was supplanted in the Queen's affections by Mrs Abigail Masham, a poor relation of her own whom she had introduced into the household. Her jealousy turned to fury when she found that the Tory leaders used Mrs Masham as an instrument against her husband and the Whig administration. A sign of the changing relationship came in 1708 when Prince George lay dying in Kensington. Sarah travelled through the night to be with Anne, who welcomed her 'very coolly and like a stranger'.

Prince George, a plump and bibulous Dane, saw himself as a martial man, but his contemporaries would not employ him as such. 'I have tried him drunk,' said Charles II, 'and I have tried him sober and there is nothing in him.' Charles, a dedicated weight-watcher, had looked askance at the Prince's bulging waistcoat. 'Walk with me, hunt with my brother, and do justice to my niece,' he told the young man, 'and you will never be fat.' George's corpulence and incompetence, however, made no difference to his wife's affections: Anne adored him. After he died she was distraught. Sarah did her best to comfort the

Queen, persuading her to move out of Kensington and into St James's to get away from what she coldly called 'that dismal body'. Before leaving, Anne told the Lord Treasurer to 'give directions that there may be a great many yeomen of the guard to carry the Prince's dear body, that it may not fall, the great stairs being very steep and slippery'.

After a few more years of strained conversations and scenes, Sarah and Anne faced each other in the Queen's suite at Kensington. Sarah, who was already furious at being kept waiting in an outside room by some minor court official 'like a Scotch lady with a petition waiting for an answer', sailed into the attack at once with her loaded guns, firing broadside after broadside. Anne, not noted for swift repartee, countered this storm of recriminations, reproaches and requests by obstinately repeating over and over again that Sarah should put what she had to say into writing. 'You said you desire no answer and I shall give you none.' Amid her tears and sobs Sarah could think eventually of nothing better to say than that Anne would suffer for her inhumanity. 'That will be to myself,' replied the Queen stiffly. From that April day in 1710 until her death nearly four years later she never set eyes on Sarah again.

George I decided that Kensington needed enlarging to make it more regal. His architect, William Benson, added a suite of ornate state rooms. Then the weary old Jacobean house, which had all along formed the centre of the palace, gave place to the Cube or Cupola Room, which had Drawing Rooms on either side. Vanbrugh, Wren's successor as Surveyor-General, produced the plans while society's arbiter of good taste, William Kent, designed the interior decorations in the style of Imperial Rome: Ionic columns, gilded statues of classical gods and goddesses, marble floors and heavy chandeliers. But their building was a grand salute to the new Hanoverian occupant of the throne. On the ceiling Kent had painted a Garter Star, that great symbol of regal continuity in England.

It was William Kent who transformed Wren's King's Staircase into the Grand Staircase, leading into the richly decorated Presence Chamber. Upon the walls and ceiling he painted groups of people looking out over a marble balustrade to welcome the King: Mahomet and Mustapha, two Turks who had saved George's life at the Siege of Vienna in 1685 and were rewarded by being made his paid servants for the rest of their lives; Christian Ulrich Jorry, the court dwarf; Peter the Wild Boy, who had been found aged about thirteen living like a wild animal in the woods near Hamelin and brought to England; and more conventional figures, such as some Yeomen of the Guard. On the ceiling Kent painted himself, accompanied by a lady supposed to be an actress called Elizabeth Butler — his intimate companion — gazing down at a scene which he had no doubt hoped would proclaim forever his own artistic triumph as well as the glory of George I.

Towards the end of his reign, George gave orders to Henry Wise to prepare plans for landscaping the gardens south of the palace. These designs, in which Kent had a hand as well, served to guide the gardeners of the second Hanoverian monarch. Their wider changes gave us much of Hyde Park and Kensington Gardens as we know them today. The Round Pond and the Serpentine, made by linking up six ponds, provided those vistas of water which belonged to the new concept of what English gardens should be. The earth from them formed an artificial mound — long since gone — which supported a revolving summerhouse much favoured by Queen Caroline, wife of George II. A delightful little building known as the Queen's Temple stood in the south-east corner of the gardens, while some 330 acres of Hyde Park were fenced for a royal menagerie. The King opened these gardens to the public on Saturdays, the day he and his court went to Hampton. The broad walks leading to the palace saw throngs of people that day as it became fashionable to promenade at Kensington. Thomas Tickell had the gardens in mind when in 1722 he wrote:

> *The dames of Britain oft in crowds repair*
> *To gravel walks, and unpolluted air.*
> *Here, while the Town in damps and darkness lies,*
> *They breathe in sunshine, and see azure skies.*

George II liked Kensington as much as his father had done. Lord Hervey gives us one or two glimpses of this peppery little military man. Details could infuriate him. As the Princess Royal told Hervey: 'When great points go as he would not have them, he frets and is bad to himself; but when he is in his worst humours, and the devil to everybody that comes near him, it is always because one of his pages has powdered his periwig ill, or a housemaid set a chair where it does not use to stand, or something of that kind.' What an impossible man!

Once Hervey, acting on the Queen's instructions, moved some indifferent pictures out of the great Drawing Room at Kensington and replaced them with better ones. The King told him the Van Dyck's could remain, but, he added, 'the picture with the dirty frame over the door, and the three nasty children [probably Van Dyck's painting of Charles I's family] I will have them taken away…' Hervey ventured to say, 'Would your Majesty have the gigantic fat Venus restored too?' George replied, 'Yes, my lord, I am not so nice as your Lordship. I like my fat Venus much better than anything you have given me instead of her.'

Hervey carried this news back to Queen Caroline and her children and barely had he finished his report when the King came in and in one of his most peevish and snappish moods proceeded to bark at the company like a Hanoverian drill sergeant. He 'snubbed the Queen, who was drinking chocolate, for being always stuffing, the Princess Emily for not hearing him, the Princess Caroline for being grown fat, the Duke [of Cumberland] for standing awkwardly, Lord Hervey for not knowing what relation the Prince of Sultzbach was to the Elector Palatine, and then carried the Queen to walk, and be resnubbed, in the garden.'

The King was equally insensitive to the Queen about his mistresses, whom she chose to overlook. If Hervey is to be believed, he once sought his wife's help in a letter forty pages long to assist him to have an affair with the Princess of Modena, whom he had not met. It was more difficult for Caroline to ignore Mrs Howard (later Lady Suffolk), for she was one of her 'women of the bedchamber'. The Queen declined to pay Mr Howard blackmail money of £1,200 a year 'to let his wife stay with me'.

Despite such treatment, George was deeply devoted to Caroline. He recognized her goodness and valued her intelligence. For she was a woman of sensibility and wide intellectual interests, which embraced theology and philosophy. Sir Isaac Newton lived in Kensington in his old age and Queen Caroline often conversed with him for hours at a stretch. She said that it made her happy to have known so great a man. When this most attractive woman died at St James's in 1737 the King was stricken by grief and remorse from which he never fully recovered.

After George II's own death from an apoplectic fit in 1760, the palace ceased to be a residence of the sovereign. Apart from the state rooms, the buildings were divided into houses or apartments for members of the royal family. George III, for example, allowed his sixth son, the Duke of Sussex, to live in the south wing. His fourth son, the Duke of Kent, and his wife Princess Victoria of Leiningen, eventually occupied the two floors beneath the state rooms, a 'favour' dwelling granted him by George IV without too much 'grace'. The Duke was sure that his 'plump as a partridge' baby daughter, Princess Victoria, born here on 24 May 1819, would one day sit on the throne. 'Take care of her, for she will be Queen of England,' he would say.

The baby was christened in the Cupola Room upstairs. The Prince Regent proved to be an unpredictable godfather when it came to announcing the list of her names. He shook his head violently when the Duke whispered 'Charlotte', the name of his dead daughter. Neither would 'Augusta' do — it sounded too grandiose. At last, while the baby weighed ever heavier in the Archbishop of Canterbury's arms, he grumpily announced 'Alexandrina'. After a long pause he added, 'Let her be called after her mother'. As, by his order, Alexandrina was her first name they called her Drina until her ninth year. After the Duke of Kent's death a few months later, the Duchess and her husband's equerry, Sir John Conroy, brought up Victoria in Kensington Palace.

Victoria's childhood was lived in an emotionally charged atmosphere, as unhappy in its way as the early years of Queen Elizabeth I. Victoria herself described it as 'rather melancholy'. Quite what relationship Conroy enjoyed with her mother is unknown, but Victoria looked upon him as a domineering, deceitful, even cruel man. Baroness Lehzen, her tutor, had a fierce devotion to her and provided the best, if somewhat strict, influences upon her upbringing. The Duchess, the third side in the triangle tugging for her affections, enjoyed her daughter's respect but not much more. 'I don't believe Ma ever really loved me,' Victoria once told Lord Melbourne.

When she was eleven Victoria learnt that she stood next to William in line of succession to her uncle George. In a history lesson the Baroness once showed her a list of the kings and queens of England, with her name after George IV and William IV at the end of it. She burst into tears, but when the 'little storm' had subsided, she raised a finger and resolved solemnly, 'I will be good'. The story illustrates Victoria's sense of dedication, which always touched the hearts of her elders.

The Duchess annexed some more rooms on the first floor at Kensington, without royal permission. This unwelcome assertion of her daughter's status infuriated George IV, who publicly snubbed her for it at Windsor Castle. 'Our bedroom is very large and lofty,' wrote Victoria approvingly, 'and is very nicely furnished, then comes a little room for the maid, and a dressing-room for Mamma; then comes the old [King's] gallery which is partitioned into three large, lofty, fine and cheerful rooms. One only of these is ready furnished; it is my sitting-room and is *very* prettily furnished indeed. The next is my study, and the last is an anteroom.'

King William IV seems to have liked his niece and heir; he certainly wanted to see more of her. The old admiral-king believed, incidentally, that the sailors would take to tattooing Victoria's face and name on their arms in the belief that she had been called after Nelson's flagship *Victory* rather than a German princess! On her eighteenth birthday he offered her £10,000 a year and independence from her mother and Sir John Conroy. The letter caused a scene at Kensington, with Victoria retiring hurt to her room. 'Felt very miserable and agitated. Did not go down to dinner,' she wrote. Conroy replied on her behalf, accepting the money and declining the independence, a reply which did not fool the old King for one minute. 'Victoria has not written that letter,' he said. It was obvious, he added, that 'the Duchess and King John want money'.

In May 1836, however, a better hope for a life of her own beyond the gates of Kensington appeared in the shape of a potential suitor. That year her handsome cousin, Prince Albert of Saxe-Coburg, visited the palace. Albert was so 'full of goodness and sweetness, and very clever and intelligent', she noted. On 1 June Albert wrote to his stepmother, 'Dear aunt is very kind to us and does everything she can to please us, and our cousin also is very amiable.'

William IV died at Windsor in the early hours of 20 June 1837. As dawn broke, the Lord Chamberlain, the Marquess of Conyngham and the Archbishop of Canterbury arrived in haste by carriage from Windsor with the news. Only when they demanded to see 'the Queen' would the Duchess consent to awaken her daughter. Eventually at six o'clock Victoria came down the back stairs in dressing-gown and slippers. The Lord Chamberlain advanced to make known his errand, but no sooner did he utter the words, 'Your Majesty', than she instantly put out her hand that he might kiss it before proceeding further. At eleven that morning she held her first Privy Council in Kensington Palace. Before evening she had dismissed Conroy from her Household and twice seen her Prime Minister, Lord Melbourne, 'of course *quite alone* as I shall *always* do all my Ministers'. That night her bed was removed from her mother's room (where she had always slept) and moved to a separate room.

On 13 July Victoria finally said goodbye to her childhood home. She confided to her journal her mixed feelings:

It was the last time that I had slept in this poor old Palace, as I go to Buckingham Palace today. Though I rejoice to go into B.P. for many reasons, it is not without feelings of regret that I shall bid adieu for ever (that is to say for ever as a dwelling), to this my birth-place, where I have been born and bred, and to which I am really attached... I have gone through painful and disagreeable scenes here, 'tis true, but still I am fond of the poor old Palace... the poor rooms look so sad and deserted, everything being taken away.

Queen Victoria continued the practice of granting accommodation in the palace to members of the royal family, a benefit enjoyed today by her descendants. In 1875 she visited her sixth child, Princess Louise, who lived in Kensington (she died there in 1934). The sight of the familiar rooms brought the past vividly to mind — 'a *whole* world of recollections streamed back! — I loved the old Home — tho' it often was not a very gay or even happy one! And I am happy to think one of my daughters should live in a part of it...' Later the Queen came again to unveil a statue of herself in the Broad Walk which the Princess, a sculptor, had made in her studio in the walled garden.

In her Diamond Jubilee year of 1897 Queen Victoria decided that the state rooms should be restored and opened to the public, perhaps to enable her subjects to share her memories of 'the poor old Palace' of Kensington.

10: BUCKINGHAM PALACE

The King's house in Pimlico

Buckingham Palace in 1837, before the removal of Marble
Arch and the construction of the east wing.

When George IV inspected the half-finished conversion of his
parents' old house in Pimlico, he sent for the architect. 'Nash,'
he said, 'the state apartments you have made for me are so
handsome that I think I shall hold my courts there.' Nash
looked uncomfortable. He attempted to explain that he had
obeyed the royal direction and produced a private residence,
not a palace. 'You know nothing about the matter,' replied the
King. 'It will make an excellent palace.' But the story of
Buckingham Palace began centuries earlier — with a pair of
silk stockings.

These silk stockings were the first to be presented to Queen
Elizabeth in 1559. After a brief trial, she declared that she

would wear nothing but silk on her legs henceforth. From this beginning stemmed the royal interest in silk-making. James I looked upon it as a money-making project. He planted the land where Buckingham Palace stands today with 10,000 mulberry trees. Silkworms feeding on their leaves would, he hoped, spin a fortune for England. But the royal monopolists never established the silk industry in England, partly because by error they bought the seeds of black mulberries instead of the necessary white ones. The black variety produce delicious berries, but the silkworms will not touch them.

As London spread westwards, the overgrown Mulberry Gardens became a haunt of 'a rascally, whoring, roguing sort of people', as Samuel Pepys called them. Having surveyed the 'little company' present on the gravel walks through the rude but pretty wilderness of mulberry and whitethorn, Pepys decided to go home: 'Did not stay for a drink,' he wrote tersely in his diary. John Dryden, however, who had a weakness for eating mulberry tarts, often visited the gardens with his constant companion, the actress Mrs Reeve.

Before the Civil War, when it became clear that the royal silk industry could not be revived, a brilliant young courtier called George Goring became Keeper of the Mulberry Gardens and built for himself a small country house to the south of them on some land enclosed from the adjacent St James's Park. Lord Goring spent a small fortune in supporting King Charles in the Civil War and recalled his younger son from Paris to fight for him. 'Had I millions of crowns or scores of sons,' he wrote to his wife, 'the King and his cause should have them all.' William Lenthall, Speaker of the Long Parliament, used the house for a time during the Commonwealth period. After the Restoration, the Earl of Arlington purchased it and substantially altered it. At Arlington House, as it was now called, his countess is said to have brewed the first pot of tea ever made in England, a contribution to the nation worth a dozen victories by the redcoats. The house passed to their daughter, who had married the Duke of Grafton, Lady Castlemaine's son by Charles II. She sold it to the Duke of Devonshire, who in turn sold it to John Sheffield, Duke of Buckingham and Normanby.

Sheffield, who succeeded to his father's earldom of Mulgrave in 1658, had a varied military career. He fought in the Dutch Wars, and from commanding a troop of horse he rose to be captain of a ship of eighty-four guns; then, upon his return from sea, he became colonel of a regiment of foot. He caused offence to Charles II by entertaining hopes of the hand of Princess Anne. Swift says that he was known as the Don Juan of the court of Charles II. In 1680 he volunteered to command an expedition to punish the Moorish pirates who were besieging Tangiers. When Anne became queen she gave him his two dukedoms — a good return, it might be thought, for the love poems he wrote for her when she was seventeen.

The Duke sited his new mansion a little more to the north of the existing one, so that the central avenue of St James's Park stretched away from its front. Inside, the house had a palatial appearance. The great staircase, for example, was painted with the story of Dido. The Duke housed his library in a greenhouse, arranging his books with a novel classification system, so 'that by its mark a very Irish footman may fetch any book I want'. Beneath its windows, in the gardens laid out for him by Henry Wise, blackbirds and nightingales sang in a wilderness.

Buckingham's third wife, the illegitimate daughter of James II by Catherine Sedley, lived in the house for twenty-one years after her husband's death in 1721. Proud of her Stuart blood, she marked the anniversaries of Charles I's execution and

James II's dethronement by putting her household into black mourning clothes. In 1723, as Prince of Wales, George II approached this Jacobite 'Princess Buckingham' with intent to buy the house, but she asked £60,000 — an enormous sum in those days. She loved her semi-royal protocol. When she lay on her deathbed, the Duchess made her servants promise not to sit down in her presence until she had been pronounced absolutely dead.

Eventually, in 1762, the new owner, one of the Duke's illegitimate sons, agreed to sell Buckingham House to George III for less than half his mother's price. On 6 June that year George III moved his wife, Queen Charlotte, into the house. Twelve years later it became formally her own dower house by an Act of Parliament, in exchange for Somerset House. She redecorated the Queen's House, as it was then called, in sumptuous style. For the first time, various rooms were named after the colours of their wallpaper, such as the Crimson Drawing Room and the Blue Drawing Room. The Queen's sitting room, the Green Closet, was graced by Gainsborough's portraits of most of the royal children. George III and Queen Charlotte kept the celebrated artist busy, for they had fifteen, all but one born at Buckingham House.

The King followed an unvarying daily routine in whichever palace he stayed: morning chapel, breakfast alone, or with the Queen and the princesses seated according to seniority, a horse ride in the Park or chess on wet days, dinner at two o'clock, public business in his study, and cards in the evening until the clock struck ten. The Queen busied herself in the nursery. She even took lessons herself and was said to have made good progress in mineralogy and natural history. Thus life in the Queen's House seemed tedious to the courtiers. One observer summed it up in a nutshell: 'constant avocations without any employment, and a great deal of idleness without any leisure; many words pronounced and nothing said; many people smiling, and nobody pleased; many disappointments and little success; little grandeur and less happiness.'

The presence of royalty had to be acknowledged by obedience to a set of rules. If the door of a room occupied by one of the royal family stood open you could not walk past it. Instead of knocking on the Queen's door, the handle had to be moved instead. Gentlemen of the court wore the Windsor uniform, blue with red and gold facings. For the King's birthday party in 1762 a new court dress for the ladies — bare shoulders and stiff-bodiced gowns — had to be worn. 'The old ladies will catch their deaths,' chortled Horace Walpole. 'What dreadful discoveries will be made, both of fat and lean! I recommend to you the idea of Mrs Cavendish when half-stark.'

Various modest alterations and additions were made to the house, notably the King's Library (now part of the British Library). Dr Samuel Johnson often resorted there to browse through the leather-bound volumes. One day in February 1767 the librarian brought the King to him as he pored over some books. They discussed literature for a while. Then the King asked Johnson if he was writing anything himself at present. Johnson remarked that he thought he had written quite enough already. 'I should have thought so too,' replied George, 'if you had not written so well.' Later Johnson would often repeat this handsome compliment to his friends and acquaintances. One asked him if he made any reply. 'No, Sir,' said Johnson in his sonorous voice. 'When the King had said it, it was to be so. It was not for me to bandy civilities with my Sovereign.'

Today there is no more popular sight than the Changing of the Guard at Buckingham Palace. In George III's reign the red-coated guardsmen were called upon to defend their sovereign on one occasion. A storm gathered and came to a head in June 1780 in the Gordon Riots, the most formidable popular rising of the 18th century, when 'anti-popery' agitators whipped up a mob of about 50,000 in St George's Fields in London. A brigade of soldiers, quartered in the 40-acre garden, stood ready to resist the armed crowds as they surged towards Westminster. George walked among the soldiers and, seeing that no bedding had been provided, he said: 'My lads, my crown cannot purchase you straw tonight, but depend on it, I have given orders that a sufficiency shall be here tomorrow forenoon.' In the meantime his servants would issue them with wine and spirits, 'and I shall keep you company till morning'. He visited the sentries all night and kept the officers company in the Riding School. Next morning, when some of the mob were sighted entering St James's Park, the King ordered the soldiers to keep them off with fixed bayonets but on no account to fire. Such resolute action on his part contributed to the collapse of the rising.

After his accession, George IV decided to move from Carlton House to 'the King's house in Pimlico', as it became known. He commissioned John Nash to transform the house into a palace. 'I am too old to build a palace,' he told Nash. 'If the Public wish to have a palace, I have no objection to build one, but I must have a *pied-à-terre*.' Nash built for him the most splendid *pied-à-terre* in London. Of course the public did not want to pay for the new palace which, as Nash at first proposed, would be on a site aligned with Pall Mall. Nor did they wish to see a palace of 'unnecessary splendour' raised in the capital, or so the critics said. Be that as it may, Nash soon spent the £200,000 voted by Parliament in 1825 'for repairs and fitments' to the old house, and came back for more money — and more.

Nash constructed a palace consisting of a main building incorporating the old house, together with two low wings extending eastwards and ending in lofty pillared loggias. The latter looked so odd that they were subsequently dismantled. Critics also poured scorn on the sight of the dome in the garden block, which was visible above the entrance portico in the east front, looking like a 'wretched inverted egg-cup'. Inside the house, Nash refashioned the entrance into the Grand Hall. The Grand Staircase in marble led up to the Picture Gallery. Two sets of state rooms lay on either side: those on the east, facing inwards, included the Green Drawing Room and the Throne Room. Along the west front, with its graceful bow and terrace above the garden, stood such apartments as the State Dining Room, the Blue Drawing Room (then a ballroom), and the domed Music Room in the bow. The royal private suite occupied the first floor of the north wing.

To justify Nash's estimates for 1829 for the 'New Palace in St James's Park' it was put about that once it was finished St James's would be demolished. As an economy measure, Nash promised to use as many materials as possible from the dismantled Carlton House. Yet his grand entrance between the arms of the two wings, the Marble Arch inspired by the Arch of Constantine in Rome, cost nearly £35,000, though it had a secondary function as a war memorial to the fallen heroes of Trafalgar and Waterloo. The statue of George IV designed for the top of this arch stood unfinished in the studio of Sir Francis Chantrey at the King's death; eventually Parliament paid the sculptor's bill and erected it in Trafalgar Square.

William IV lacked any enthusiasm for Nash's buildings, although work continued upon the unfinished edifice. If the government wished it, William said, he would move to

Buckingham House, 'tho' he thinks it a most ill-contrived house; and if he goes there, he hopes it may be *plain*, and no gilding, for he dislikes it extremely.' He would have preferred to live in Marlborough House, linked by an underground passage to St James's Palace. What could he do with Buckingham House? The sale of this 'Pimlico palace' was mooted; the King even offered it as a home for Parliament after the great fire of 1838 which destroyed Westminster Palace. Then William toyed with the idea of turning it into a barracks for the regiments of Foot Guards. But in the end he reluctantly agreed to make it his London residence.

While workmen hammered, painted, moved furniture and installed gas lighting in preparation for the move, the diarist Thomas Creevey was given a conducted tour. One of the growing army of critics, he clearly shared William's estimate of the place:

> It has cost a million of money, and there is not a fault that has not been committed in it… Instead of being called Buckingham Palace it should be called the Brunswick Hotel. The costly ornaments of the State Rooms exceed all belief in their bad taste… Raspberry coloured pillars without end, that quite turn you sick to look at; but the Queen's papers for her own apartments far exceed everything else in their ugliness and vulgarity.

Those thirty rose-coloured columns in the Blue Drawing Room are now painted to resemble onyx!

Death excused William IV from living in these ornate surroundings. Queen Victoria, however, had no hesitation. A fortnight after her accession she removed in the state coach from Kensington to Buckingham Palace, the name she chose for it. 'I am much-pleased with my rooms,' she wrote. 'They are high, pleasant and cheerful.' The furniture was incomplete and the carpets not down. Only a few of the fifty new lavatories worked and one of these emptied on to the lead roof beneath the Queen's bedroom. A main sewer which ran under the kitchen could overflow on occasions and seep above the floor. As the plumbers tackled these problems, other workmen carried out urgent alterations, such as knocking a door into the Queen's bedroom wall so that Victoria's 'dearest Daisy', Baroness Lehzen, could have immediate access to her former charge. At this time also, her architects removed the unsuccessful central dome from the palace roof. Within three months she held her first state concert in Buckingham Palace.

Court life transplanted, Buckingham Palace soon settled down to the familiar pattern of a humdrum social routine enlivened with the occasional scandal. The young Queen presided pleasantly over gatherings which required no more from her than the smallest of small talk and a gracious smile. Charles Greville, who attended a dinner party at Buckingham Palace in January 1838, stood with the other men near the door of the drawing room 'in the sort of half-shy, half-awkward way people do'. Victoria came to talk to each in turn. 'Have you been riding today, Mr Greville?' she asked. 'No, Madam, I have not.' The Queen: 'It was a fine day.' Greville: 'Yes, ma'am, a very fine day.' The Queen: 'It was rather cold though.' Greville: 'It *was* rather cold, madam.' And so on.

In November 1839 an event occurred which promised to transform the life of the court at Buckingham Palace. To an assembly of eighty-two Privy Councillors in the Bow Room the Queen, dressed in a plain morning gown, read out her intention of marrying Prince Albert of Saxe-Coburg. Greville, Clerk of the Privy Council, noted that she read the words in 'a clear, sonorous, sweet-toned voice, but her hands trembled so excessively that I wonder she was able to read the paper which she held.' Before she had walked into the Bow Room, someone had asked her if she felt nervous. 'Yes, but I did a much more nervous thing a little while ago,' she said. 'What was that?' Victoria replied: 'I proposed to Prince Albert.'

After their marriage, Prince Albert and Queen Victoria certainly livened up the court for a while. They danced together, waltzing round the crowded ballroom. They performed together on two pianos at grand concerts held in the palace. At the Queen's Plantagenet Ball in May 1842, one of a series of three fancy-dress balls, they appeared as Edward III and Philippa. But the third ball — in Stuart costume — proved to be the last of such extravagances. For the Queen and Prince Albert formed a dislike for life in London. In the quest for family privacy they looked elsewhere for more secluded homes. Even Windsor Castle, joined to the capital by the Great Western Railway, became less agreeable to them as time went on. Towards the end of the reign, Buckingham Palace had acquired the air of an official palace and the Queen's annual visits were as short as her supreme sense of duty would allow.

Perhaps the eventual desire of Victoria and Albert to escape as often as possible from Buckingham Palace is understandable when one contemplates the peculiar social behaviour generated by the presence of the sovereign. Within the enclosed world of the court and the royal family, competitive feelings sometimes boil over with intensity, as imperfect humans are exposed to the charisma of royalty, an attraction felt often regardless of the personality of a particular sovereign.

Sometimes historical fact surpasses even the best fiction. At the wedding in Buckingham Palace of Princess Augusta of Cambridge to a German grand duke in 1843, those royal dukes who had always resented the precedence given to Prince Albert found a worthy champion to take the lists against the 'paper

Royal Highness'. Those 'infernal scoundrels', as Victoria called them, watched with glee as their brother Ernest, now King of Hanover, pushed Albert aside so that he could sign the register after the Queen.

Prince Albert described the events in a letter to his brother:

> *It almost came to a fight with the King. He insisted on having the place at the altar, where we stood. He wanted to drive me away, and, against all custom, he wanted to accompany Victoria and lead her. I was forced to give him a strong punch and drive him down a few steps, where the First Master of Ceremonies took him and led him out of the Chapel. We have a second scene, where he would not allow me to sign the register with Victoria. He laid his fist on the book. We manoeuvred round the table and Victoria had the book handed to her across the table. Now the table was between us and he could see what was being done. After a third trial to force Victoria to do what he commanded, but in vain, he left the party in great wrath. Since then we let him go, and, happily, he fell over some stones in Kew and damaged some ribs.*

As Victoria bore more children, the deficiencies of Buckingham Palace as a family home became more apparent. In 1845 she reminded Sir Robert Peel in a letter about 'the urgent necessity of doing something to Buckingham Palace… and the total want of accommodation for our little family, which is fast growing up.' Most parts of the palace were in a sad state, needing a further outlay 'to render them *decent* for the occupation of the Royal Family or any visitors the Queen may have to receive'. Measures would have to be taken also 'to render the exterior of the Palace such as no longer to be a *disgrace* in the country'. The Prime Minister proved sympathetic and next year Parliament voted the necessary funds, laying it down as a condition that the Royal Pavilion at Brighton should be sold to defray the expense.

Under the directions of her architect, Sir Edward Blore, the builders erected a new east front, thus completing the quadrangle. It is like a stone veil of privacy across the face and outstretched arms of the old house. To make way for it they moved the Marble Arch to the site of the old gallows at Tyburn, where it began a new career as a traffic island. The wide balcony on the east front was ready in time for Victoria to stand there and watch the Scots and Coldstream Guards parade in front of her before marching off to embark for the Crimea. 'They formed line, presented arms and then cheered us very heartily, and went off cheering,' wrote Victoria to her uncle King Leopold. 'It was a touching and beautiful sight.'

In that same year, Sir James Pennethorne, a pupil of John Nash, began work upon some interior alterations. He replaced the Armoury and Octagon Library of George III with the new Ballroom. A throne dais occupied one end and an organ (from Brighton Pavilion) stood at the other end. Today it is the scene of investitures and state banquets. By 1856, when the Ballroom was finished, Queen Victoria was on the balcony once more, welcoming home the Guards from the Crimea. As 20,000 British soldiers had succumbed in two years in that disease-ridden corner of Russia, the ranks of the Foot Guards looked much thinner.

Soon war broke out in the lands once ruled by Queen Victoria's grandfather. In 1870 Charles Dickens brought back with him from America some photographs of the famous Civil War battlefields, such as Bull Run and Gettysburg, which the Queen asked to see. When she summoned Dickens to Buckingham Palace to thank him for sending them to her, he requested permission to present her with a bound set of his books. In reply Victoria picked up her own *Leaves from the Journal of Our Life in the Highlands* and autographed it, saying that 'as one of the humblest writers' she felt ashamed to offer it to 'one of the greatest'. She later recorded Dickens's opinion that the division of classes would gradually cease. 'And I earnestly pray that it may,' she added.

Although Queen Victoria excluded Prince Albert from all affairs of state, he found plenty to occupy his intelligent mind. Among other things, he took an interest in the day-to-day running of the palace, which exhibited some perennial characteristics of English working life alien to his German passion for efficiency and cleanliness. One servant, for example, collected all the tallow candles every day, which he then sold, as one of his perks. George III had once ordered the candles to cure a cold and since then hundreds of them had been placed and removed as part of the daily ritual. The Lord Steward's staff were supposed to lay the fires, while the Lord Chamberlain's staff had the job of lighting them: a recipe for a cold palace. Two different departments were responsible for cleaning the insides and outsides of the windows. Sensibly, Prince Albert grouped all the palace staff under a resident Master of the Household.

When Albert died in 1861 Victoria lived mainly at Windsor, which was as close to the capital as she cared to be. Dust sheets over the furniture in Buckingham Palace gave it a funereal air. The Prince's rooms remained unchanged. When Victoria stayed at the palace on rare occasions, the servants laid out her dead husband's evening clothes as they did each night at Windsor. In 1873 the Queen lent the palace to the Shah of Persia during his state visit. His Eastern habits caused her much annoyance. The Shah ate his meals on the floor, which did the carpets no good. Women of dubious reputation kept him company. According to one report, he had a servant strangled with a bowstring and his corpse burned in the gardens. Certainly he watched a prize-fight in the palace grounds. It was all very different from the romantic vision of court life in the paradise of a cool Eastern palace that had inspired Victoria's uncle to build his Pavilion at Brighton.

The palace remained lifeless during the closing decades of Victoria's reign, save for the celebrations of her Golden and Diamond Jubilees. In 1900 the Queen returned there for the last time. Twenty or thirty thousand joyful Londoners serenaded her when news of the relief of Ladysmith reached the capital. On the night of 9 March, in response to the surging crowds, she appeared on the balcony to acknowledge their ovations. In the forecourt of the palace on the following day she reviewed 2,000 of the Guards who were leaving for South Africa.

Victoria's son, King Edward VII, made the last changes in Buckingham Palace. His architect, Sir Aston Webb, began the work of replacing the crumbling Caen stone on the east front with nearly 6,000 tons of Portland stone. He altered the face to make it a plain, dignified backcloth to the memorial to Queen Victoria which was to stand in front of the palace. Sir Thomas Block designed this Victoria Memorial, which included Motherhood in the Queen's virtues there commemorated. At the other end of the Mall, Webb built the Admiralty Arch as a grand entrance to the processional way.

Their work completed the story of how a country house amid a garden of mulberry trees became the principal palace of the monarch in London.

SELECT BIBLIOGRAPHY

Bell, W. G., *The Tower of London* (1921)

Chettle, G. H., *The Queen's House, Greenwich* (1937)

Chettle, G. H., *Hampton Court Palace* (1954)

Clifford, H., *Buckingham Palace* (1931)

Douglas-Irvine, Helen, *Royal Palaces of Scotland* (1911)

Dugdale, G. S., *Whitehall through the Centuries* (1950)

Harris, John, de Bellaigue, Geoffrey and Millar, Oliver, *Buckingham Palace* intr. John Russell (1968)

Hedley, Olwen, *Windsor Castle* (1967)

Hedley, Olwen, *Royal Palaces: An Account of the Homes of British Sovereigns from Saxon to Modern Times* (1972)

Hibbert, Christopher, *Tower of London* (1972)

Hibbert, Christopher, *The Court at Windsor: A Domestic History* (2nd ed. 1980)

Howard, Philip, *The Royal Palaces* (1970)

Hudson, Derek, *Kensington Palace* (1968)

Lindsay, Philip, *Hampton Court: A History* (1948)

Morshead, Sir Owen, *Windsor Castle* (2nd ed. 1957)

Musgrave, Clifford, *The Royal Pavilion* (1959)

Pyne, W. H., *The History of the Royal Residences* (1829)

Rowse, A. L., *Windsor Castle in the History of the Nation* (1974)

Shepphard, Edgar, *Memorials of St James's Palace* (1894)

Williams, Neville, *The Royal Residences of Great Britain* (1960)

A NOTE TO THE READER

If you have enjoyed this book enough to leave a review on **Amazon** and **Goodreads**, then I would be truly grateful.

John Adair

Sapere Books is an exciting new publisher of brilliant fiction and popular history.

To find out more about our latest releases and our monthly bargain books visit our website:
saperebooks.com

Printed in Great Britain
by Amazon

63774226R00095